GCSE
Success

Biology

Tom
Adams

Revision Guide

Contents

Coordination and Control

Inheritance, Variation and Evolution

Ecosystems

Answers

Cells are the basis of life. All processes of life take place within them. There are many different kinds of specialised cell but they all have several common features. The two main categories of cells are **prokaryotic** (prokaryotes) and **eukaryotic** (eukaryotes).

Structure of cells

Prokaryotes

Prokaryotes are simple cells such as bacteria and archaebacteria. Archaebacteria are ancient bacteria with different types of cell wall and genetic codes to other bacteria. They include microorganisms that can use methane or sulfur as a means of nutrition (methanogens and thermoacidophiles).

Prokaryotic cells:

➤ are smaller than eukaryotic cells
➤ have cytoplasm, a cell membrane and a cell wall
➤ have genetic material in the form of a DNA loop, together with rings of DNA called plasmids
➤ do not have a nucleus.

The chart below shows the relative sizes of prokaryotic and eukaryotic cells, together with the magnification range of different viewing devices.

A bacterium

Plasmid DNA: a small, commonly circular, section of DNA that can replicate independently of chromosomal DNA

Ribosomes: sites of protein manufacture

Chromosomal DNA: the DNA of bacteria is not found within a nucleus and is usually found as one circular chromosome

Cytoplasm

Cell wall: provides structural support to the bacteria (is not made of cellulose)

Flagella: tail-like structures that rotate to help some bacteria move

| 1 nm | 10 nm | 100 nm | 1 µm | 10 µm | 100 µm | 1 mm |

Prokaryotic cells   Eukaryotic cells

Eye — Visible with

Light microscope — Visible with

Electron microscope — Visible with

Eukaryotes

Eukaryotic cells:

➤ are more complex than prokaryotic cells (they have a cell membrane, cytoplasm and genetic material enclosed in a nucleus)

➤ are found in animals, plants, fungi (e.g. toadstools, yeasts, moulds) and protists (e.g. amoeba)

➤ contain membrane-bound structures called **organelles**, where specific functions are carried out.

Here are the main organelles in plant and animal cells.

Human cheek cell (typical animal cell)

Palisade cell (typical plant cell)

Mitochondrion: where aerobic respiration takes place

Cell membrane: controls movement into and out of the cell; contains receptor molecules and is a selective barrier

Cytoplasm: chemical reactions take place here

Nucleus: controls what the cell does and contains the genetic information

Ribosome: where protein synthesis occurs

Cellulose cell wall: strengthens and supports the cell

Chloroplast: contains chlorophyll and absorbs light for photosynthesis

Permanent vacuole: filled with cell sap, it helps to support the cell

Plant cells tend to be more regular in shape than animal cells. They have additional structures: cell wall, sap vacuole and sometimes chloroplasts.

Keyword

Organelle ➤ A membrane-bound structure within a cell that carries out a particular function

Create a poster illustrating the main features of bacterial, plant and animal cells (i.e. prokaryotes and eukaryotes).

➤ Use different colours for the main organelles, e.g. blue for the nucleus, orange for cytoplasm.

➤ Add labels that describe the functions of the organelles.

1. List three examples of prokaryotes and three examples of eukaryotes.
2. How are prokaryotes and eukaryotes different in terms of genetic information?
3. All cells have a cell membrane. True or false?
4. Which organelle carries out the function of respiration?
5. Algae are a type of plant. Why do the cells contain chloroplasts?

Organisation and differentiation

Multicellular organisms need to have a coordinated system of structures so they can carry out vital processes, e.g. respiration, excretion, nutrition, etc.

Principles of organisation

Cells are the most basic unit of living organisms.

Tissues are collections of similar cells that work together to carry out the same function.

An organ is formed when a group of tissues combine together and do a particular job.

Organs form organ systems, e.g. the intestines and the stomach are part of the digestive system.

Organ systems work together to make up a complex multicellular organism.

Organisation

Cell specialisation

Animals and plants have many different types of cells. Each cell is adapted to carry out a specific function. Some cells can act independently, e.g. white blood cells, but most operate together as tissues.

Type of specialised animal cell	How they are adapted
Sperm cells	➤ They are adapted for swimming in the female reproductive system – mitochondria in the neck release energy for swimming. ➤ They are adapted for carrying out fertilisation with an egg cell – the acrosome contains enzymes for digestion of the ovum's outer protective cells at fertilisation.
Egg cells (ovum)	➤ They are very large in order to carry food reserves for the developing embryo. ➤ After fertilisation, the cell membrane changes and locks out other sperm.
Ciliated epithelial cells	➤ They line the respiratory passages and help protect the lungs against dust and microorganisms.
Nerve cells	➤ They have long, slender extensions called axons that carry nerve impulses.
Muscle cells	➤ They are able to contract (shorten) to bring about the movement of limbs.

Type of specialised plant cell	How they are adapted
Root hair cells	➤ They have tiny, hair-like extensions. These increase the surface area of roots to help with the absorption of water and minerals.
Xylem	➤ They are long, thin, hollow cells. Their shape helps with the transport of water through the stem, roots and leaves.
Phloem	➤ They are long, thin cells with pores in the end walls. Their structure helps the cell sap move from one phloem cell to the next.

Cell differentiation and stem cells

Stem cells are found in animals and plants. They are unspecialised or **undifferentiated**, which means that they have the potential to become almost any kind of cell. Once the cell is fully specialised, it will possess sub-cellular organelles specific to the function of that cell. Embryonic stem cells, compared with those found in adults' bone marrow, are more flexible in terms of what they can become.

Animal cells are mainly restricted to repair and replacement in later life. Plants retain their ability to **differentiate** (specialise) throughout life.

Using stem cells in humans

Therapeutic cloning treats conditions such as diabetes. Embryonic stem cells (that can specialise into any type of cell) are produced with the same genes as the patient. If these are introduced into the body, they are not usually rejected.

Treating paralysis is possible using stem cells that are capable of differentiating into new nerve cells. The brain uses these new cells to transmit nervous impulses to the patient's muscles.

There are benefits and objections to using stem cells.

Benefits	Risks and objections
➤ Stem cells left over from in vitro fertilisation (IVF) treatment (that would otherwise be destroyed) can be used to treat serious conditions. ➤ Stem cells are useful in studying how cell division goes wrong, e.g. cancer. ➤ In the future, stem cells could be used to grow new organs for transplantation.	➤ Some people believe that an embryo at any age is a human being and so should not be used to grow cells or be experimented on. ➤ One potential risk of using stem cells is transferring viral infections. ➤ If stem cells are used in an operation, they might act as a reservoir of cancer cells that spread to other parts of the body.

Keywords

Haploid nucleus ➤ Nucleus with a half chromosome set

Stem cells ➤ Undifferentiated cells that can become any type of cell

Differentiation ➤ A process by which cells become specialised, i.e. have a particular structure to carry out their function

Therapeutic cloning ➤ A process where embryos are grown to produce cells with the same genes as a particular patient

Meristems ➤ Growth regions in plants where stem cells are produced, e.g. apical bud

Using stem cells in plants

Plants have regions of rapid cell division called **meristems**. These growth regions contain stem cells that can be used to produce clones cheaply and quickly.

Meristems can be used for:
➤ growing and preserving rare varieties to protect them from extinction
➤ producing large numbers of disease-resistant crop plants.

Produce a set of true/false cards with statements about cell specialisation on one side and the answers on the other. Use them with a friend to test your knowledge of the module. For example: 'All cells are able to differentiate throughout an organism's lifetime. True or false?' Answer: 'False – only plant cells can do this.'

1. In the body, what do you call an arrangement of different tissues that carry out a particular job?
2. Describe how a muscle cell is specialised to perform its function.
3. Which type of specialised plant cell is used to transport the sugars made in photosynthesis?
4. Give one benefit of and one objection to the scientific use of stem cells.

Microscopy and microorganisms

Microscopes

Microscopes:

➤ observe objects that are too small to see with the naked eye

➤ are useful for showing detail at cellular and sub-cellular level.

There are two main types of microscope: the **light microscope** and the **electron microscope**.

Light microscope

← Eye piece

Objective lenses of different magnifications

Iris

Light source

Electron microscope

You will probably use a light microscope in your school laboratory.

The electron microscope was invented in 1931. It has increased our understanding of sub-cellular structures because it has much higher magnifications and resolution than a light microscope.

These are white blood cells, as seen through a transmission electron microscope. The black structures are nuclei.

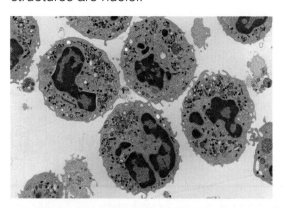

HT Here are some common units used in microscopy.

Measure	Scale	Symbol
1 metre		m
1 millimetre	$\frac{1}{1000}$ (a thousandth) of a metre ($\times 10^{-3}$)	mm
1 micrometre	$\frac{1}{1\,000\,000}$ (a millionth) of a metre ($\times 10^{-6}$)	μm
1 nanometre	$\frac{1}{1\,000\,000\,000}$ (a thousand millionth or a billionth) of a metre ($\times 10^{-9}$)	nm
1 picometre	$\frac{1}{1\,000\,000\,000\,000}$ (a million millionth or a trillionth) of a metre ($\times 10^{-12}$)	pm

Comparing light and electron microscopes

Light microscope	Electron microscope
Uses light waves to produce images	Uses electrons to produce images
Low resolution	High resolution
Magnification up to ×1500	Magnification up to ×500 000 (2D) and ×100 000 (3D)
Able to observe cells and larger organelles	Able to observe small organelles
2D images only	2D and 3D images produced

Keywords

Resolution ➤ The smallest distance between two points on a specimen that can still be told apart

Pathogen ➤ A harmful microorganism

Binary fission ➤ Process where bacterial cells divide into two

Colony ➤ A large number of microorganisms (of one type) growing in a location, e.g. a circular colony on the surface of agar

Magnification and resolution

Magnification measures how many times an object under a microscope has been made larger.

To calculate the magnifying power of a microscope, use this formula:

$$\text{magnification} = \frac{\text{size of image}}{\text{size of real object}}$$

You may be asked to carry out calculations using magnification.

> **Example:** A light microscope produces an image of a cell which has a diameter of 1500 µm. The cell's actual diameter is 50 µm. Calculate the magnifying power of the microscope.
>
> $$\text{magnification} = \frac{1500}{50} = \times 30$$

Resolution is the smallest distance between two points on a specimen that can still be told apart. The diagram below shows the limits of resolution for a light microscope. When looking through it you can see fine detail down to 200 nanometres. Electron microscopes can see detail down to 0.05 nanometres!

 200 nm

Staining techniques are used in light and electron microscopy to make organelles more visible.
> **Methylene blue** is used to stain the nuclei of animal cells for viewing under the light microscope.
> **Heavy metals** such as cadmium can be used to stain specimens for viewing under the electron microscope.

Culturing microorganisms

To view microorganisms under the microscope, pure, uncontaminated samples are grown or **cultured** in the laboratory. These cultures can be used for research, e.g. investigating the action of disinfectants or antibiotics.

In order to grow, microorganisms need:
> **food** in the form of a growth medium; in the laboratory, this is usually nutrient agar or broth
> **warmth** – a temperature of 25°C is used in school laboratories, as it lowers the possibility of **pathogens** growing
> **moisture**.

 3

Aseptic technique

Aseptic technique is needed to culture microorganisms in the laboratory so that:
> uncontaminated cultures are produced
> the risk of scientists being infected by pathogens is reduced.

Bacterial growth

Under ideal conditions, a bacterial cell will grow quickly over a period of days by **binary fission**. In this process, a cell divides into two in as little time as twenty minutes!

The bacteria continue to divide in this way: 1, 2, 4, 8, 16, 32, 64, etc. So after a day, the numbers are in their millions. As they grow, the individual cells merge to produce circular **colonies** that are visible to the naked eye. You can count them or calculate their area to estimate the growth rate.

(WS) Calculating the cross-sectional area of a bacterial colony

Bacterial colonies grow **radially**, i.e. in circles. To calculate a rate of growth, the area of the colony can be worked out at two points in time.

Example: A colony of *M. luteus* is observed growing on agar in a petri dish. The diameter is measured with a ruler and is 20 mm. Exactly 24 hours later, the colony's diameter is 30 mm. What is its growth rate?
> Area of colony for first measurement = πr^2 where $\pi = 3.14$ and $r = \frac{1}{2} \times 20$
> Area = $3.14 \times 10^2 = 314 \text{ mm}^2$
> Area of colony for second measurement = $3.14 \times 15^2 = 706.5 \text{ mm}^2$
> Rate of growth = $\frac{706.5 - 314}{24}$
> $= \mathbf{16.35 \ mm^2 \, h^{-1}}$

1. List two differences between light and electron microscopes.
2. Which three conditions are needed for microorganisms to grow?

Cell division

Multicellular organisms grow and reproduce using cell division and cell enlargement. Plants can also grow via differentiation into leaves, branches, etc.

Cell division begins from the moment of fertilisation when the zygote replicates itself exactly through **mitosis**. Later in life, an organism may use cell division to produce sex cells (**gametes**) in a different type of division called **meiosis**.

The different stages of cell division make up the **cell cycle** of an organism.

Keywords

Gamete ➤ A sex cell, i.e. sperm or egg

Daughter cells ➤ Multiple cells arising from mitosis and meiosis

Polymer ➤ Large molecule, made of repeating units called monomers

Diploid ➤ A full set of chromosomes in a cell (twice the haploid number)

Haploid ➤ A half set of chromosomes in a cell; haploid cells are either eggs or sperm

Chromosomes

Chromosomes are found in the nucleus of eukaryotic cells. They are made of DNA and carry a large number of genes. Chromosomes exist as pairs called **homologues**.

For cells to duplicate exactly, it is important that all of the genetic material is duplicated. Chromosomes take part in a sequence of events that ensures the genetic code is transmitted precisely and appears in the new **daughter cells**.

DNA replication

During the cell cycle, the genetic material (made of the **polymer** molecule, DNA) is doubled and then divided between the identical daughter cells. This process is called **DNA replication**. (See Module 29 for more information about DNA.)

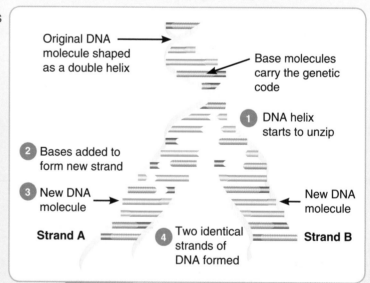

Use plasticine or playdough to create models showing mitosis and meiosis. Mitosis should show four stages and meiosis six stages.
You could:
➤ use different colours for the chromosomes and the cytoplasm
➤ try mixing the stages up and then re-arranging them from memory
➤ explain to a friend what is happening at each stage in terms of the chromosomes and cytoplasm.

Mitosis

Mitosis is where a **diploid** cell (one that has a complete set of chromosomes) divides to produce two more diploid cells that are genetically identical. Most cells in the body are diploid.

Humans have a diploid number of 46.

Mitosis produces new cells:

➤ for growth
➤ to repair damaged tissue
➤ to replace old cells
➤ for asexual reproduction.

Before the cell divides, the DNA is duplicated and other organelles replicate, e.g. mitochondria and ribosomes. This ensures that there is an exact copy of all the cell's content.

Mitosis – the cell copies itself to produce two genetically identical cells

Parent cell with two pairs of chromosomes.

Each chromosome replicates (copies) itself.

Chromosomes line up along the centre of the cell, separate into chromatids and move to opposite poles.

Each 'daughter' cell has the same number of chromosomes, and contains the same genes, as the parent cell.

Meiosis

Meiosis takes place in the testes and ovaries of sexually reproducing organisms and produces gametes (eggs or sperm). The gametes are called **haploid** cells because they contain half the number of chromosomes as a diploid cell. This chromosome number is restored during **fertilisation**.

Humans have a haploid number of 23.

Meiosis – the cell divides twice to produce four cells with genetically different sets of chromosomes

Cell with two pairs of chromosomes (diploid cell).

Each chromosome replicates itself.

Cell divides for the first time.

Chromosomes part company and move to opposite poles.

Copies now separate and the second cell division takes place.

Four haploid cells (gametes), each with half the number of chromosomes of the parent cell.

Cancer

Cancer is a non-infectious disease caused by **mutations** in living cells.

Cancerous cells:

➤ divide in an uncontrolled way
➤ form **tumours**.

Benign tumours do not spread from the original site of cancer in the body. **Malignant tumour cells** invade neighbouring tissues. They spread to other parts of the body and form **secondary tumours**.

Making healthy lifestyle choices is one way to reduce the likelihood of cancer. These include:

➤ not smoking tobacco products (cigarettes, cigars, etc.)
➤ not drinking too much alcohol (causes cancer of the liver, gut and mouth)
➤ avoiding exposure to UV rays (e.g. sunbathing, tanning salons)
➤ eating a healthy diet (high fibre reduces the risk of bowel cancer) and doing moderate exercise to reduce the risk of obesity.

Cancer cell

1. Why do multicellular organisms carry out cell division?
2. Name the structures in the nucleus that carry genetic information.
3. What are the purposes of mitosis and meiosis?
4. Which structures are replicated during cell division?

Metabolism – respiration

Metabolism

Metabolism is the sum of all the chemical reactions that take place in the body.

The two types of metabolic reaction are:
➤ building reactions (**anabolic**)
➤ breaking-down reactions (**catabolic**).

Anabolic reactions

Anabolic reactions require the input of energy. Examples include:
➤ converting glucose to starch in plants, or glucose to glycogen in animals
➤ the synthesis of lipid molecules

fatty acids + glycerol ⟶ lipids

➤ the formation of **amino acids** in plants (from glucose and nitrate ions) which, in turn, are built up into proteins.

Keywords

Exothermic reaction ➤ A reaction that gives out heat

Energy demand ➤ Energy required by tissues (particularly muscle) to carry out their functions

Oxygen debt ➤ The oxygen needed to remove lactic acid after exercise

Catabolic reactions

Catabolic reactions release energy. Examples include:
➤ breaking down amino acids to form **urea**, which is then excreted
➤ respiration.

Catabolic reactions produce waste energy in the form of heat (an **exothermic reaction**), which is transferred to the environment.

Respiration

Respiration continuously takes place in all organisms – the need to release energy is an essential life process. The reaction gives out energy and is therefore **exothermic**.

Aerobic respiration

Aerobic respiration takes place in cells. Oxygen and glucose molecules react and release energy. This energy is stored in a molecule called **ATP**.

glucose + oxygen ⟶ carbon dioxide + water

HT The symbol equation for aerobic respiration is:

$$C_6H_{12}O_6 + 6O_2 \longrightarrow 6CO_2 + 6H_2O + \text{energy released}$$

Energy is used in the body for many processes, including:
➤ muscle contraction (for movement)
➤ active transport
➤ transmitting nerve impulses
➤ synthesising new molecules
➤ maintaining a constant body temperature.

Anaerobic respiration

Anaerobic respiration takes place in the absence of oxygen and is common in muscle cells. It quickly releases a **smaller** amount of energy than aerobic respiration through the **incomplete breakdown** of glucose.

glucose ⟶ lactic acid + energy released

In plant and yeast cells, anaerobic respiration produces different products.

glucose ⟶ ethanol + carbon dioxide + energy released

HT The symbol equation for anaerobic respiration in plant and yeast cells is:

$$C_6H_{12}O_6 \longrightarrow 2C_2H_5OH + 2CO_2 + \text{energy released}$$

This reaction is used extensively in the brewing and wine-making industries. It is also the initial process in the manufacture of spirits in a distillery.

Response to exercise

In animals, anaerobic respiration takes place when muscles are working so hard that the lungs and circulatory system cannot deliver enough oxygen to break down all the available glucose through aerobic respiration. In these circumstances the **energy demand** of the muscles is high.

Anaerobic respiration and recovery

Anaerobic respiration releases energy much faster over short periods of time. It is useful when short, intense bursts of energy are required, e.g. a 100 m sprint.

However, the incomplete oxidation of glucose causes **lactic acid** to build up. Lactic acid is toxic and can cause pain, cramp and a sensation of fatigue.

The lactic acid must be broken down quickly and removed to avoid cell damage and prolonged muscle fatigue.

➤ During exercise the body's heart rate, breathing rate and breath volume increase so that sufficient oxygen and glucose is supplied to the muscles, and so that lactic acid can be removed.

➤ This continues after exercise when deep breathing or panting occurs until all the lactic acid is removed. This repayment of oxygen is called **oxygen debt**.

HT
➤ Lactic acid is transported to the liver where it is converted back to glucose.
➤ Oxygen debt is the amount of **extra** oxygen that the body needs after exercise to react with the lactic acid and remove it from the cells.

WS You may be asked to present data as graphs, tables, bar charts or histograms. For example, you could show data of breathing and heart rates on a line graph.

What does the line graph below tell you about breathing and pulse rates during recovery? Why is a line graph a good way to present the data?

---

1. Give one example of a building reaction and one of a breaking-down reaction.
2. Which type of respiration releases most energy – aerobic or anaerobic?
3. Give two uses of energy release in the body.
4. Name the products of anaerobic respiration in humans and in yeast.
5. Why do athletes pant after a race?

Metabolism – enzymes

Enzymes are **large proteins** that act as **biological** catalysts. This means they speed up chemical reactions, including reactions that take place in living cells, e.g. respiration, photosynthesis and protein synthesis.

Enzyme facts

Enzymes:

➤ are specific, i.e. one enzyme catalyses one reaction

➤ have an active site, which is formed by the precise folding of the enzyme molecule

➤ can be denatured by high temperatures and extreme changes in pH

➤ have an **optimum temperature** at which they work – for many enzymes this is approximately 37°C (body temperature)

➤ have an optimum pH at which they work – this varies with the site of enzyme activity, e.g. pepsin works in the stomach and has an optimum pH of 1.5 (acid), salivary amylase works best at pH 7.3 (alkaline).

Keywords

Catalyst ➤ A substance that controls the rate of a chemical reaction without being chemically changed itself

Active site ➤ The place on an enzyme molecule into which a substrate molecule fits

Denaturation ➤ When a protein molecule such as an enzyme changes shape and makes it unable to function

Substrate ➤ The molecule acted on by an enzyme

Kinetic energy ➤ Energy possessed by moving objects, e.g. reactant molecules such as enzyme and substrate molecules

Enzyme activity

Enzyme molecules work by colliding with **substrate** molecules and forcing them to break up or to join with others in synthesis reactions. The theory of how this works is called the **lock and key theory**.

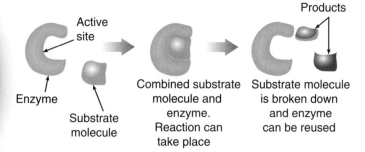

Enzyme / Active site / Substrate molecule / Combined substrate molecule and enzyme. Reaction can take place / Substrate molecule is broken down and enzyme can be reused / Products

High temperatures denature enzymes because excessive heat vibrates the atoms in the protein molecule, putting a strain on the bonds and breaking them. This changes the shape of the active site.

Enzyme / Heat / Enzyme destroyed by heat

In a similar way, an extreme pH alters the active site's shape and prevents it from functioning.

Enzyme / Substrate molecule / pH level altered / Active site / Active site changed irreversibly

At lower than the optimal temperature, an enzyme still works but much more slowly. This is because the low **kinetic energy** of the substrate and enzyme molecules lowers the number of collisions that take place. When they do collide, the energy is not always sufficient to create a bond between them.

Optimum enzyme activity / Enzyme activity / Optimum temperature / Temperature

Enzymes in the digestive system

Enzymes in the digestive system help break down large nutrient molecules into smaller ones so they can be absorbed into the blood across the wall of the small intestine.

Enzyme types in the digestive system include carbohydrases, proteases and lipases.

Carbohydrases break down carbohydrates, e.g. **amylase**, which is produced in the mouth and small intestine.

starch ⟶ maltose

Other carbohydrases break down complex sugars into smaller sugars.

Proteases break down protein, e.g. **pepsin**, which is produced in the stomach.

protein ⟶ peptides ⟶ amino acids

Other enzymes in the small intestine complete protein breakdown with the production of amino acids.

Lipases, which are produced in the small intestine, break down lipids.

lipid ⟶ fatty acids + glycerol

Bile

Bile is a digestive chemical. It is produced in the liver and stored in the gall bladder.
➤ Its alkaline pH neutralises hydrochloric acid that has been produced in the stomach.
➤ It **emulsifies** fat, breaking it into small droplets with a large surface area.
➤ Its action enables lipase to break down fat more efficiently.

What happens to digested food?

Calorimetry

Enzyme-controlled metabolic reactions such as respiration release energy. The amount of energy contained in a substrate can be measured using **calorimetry**.

The substrate (food) is placed in a calorimeter and burned in pure oxygen. The energy released heats up the surrounding water and the temperature rise is measured.

The energy released per gram can be calculated.

$$\text{energy (J)} = \text{mass of water heated (g)} \times 4.2 \times \text{temperature rise (°C)}$$

WS During your course you will investigate how certain factors affect the rate of enzyme activity. These include temperature, pH and substrate concentration.

Design an investigation to discover how temperature affects the activity of amylase. Here are some guidelines.
➤ Iodine solution turns from a red-brown colour to blue-black in the presence of starch.
➤ You can measure amylase activity by timing how long it takes for iodine solution to stop turning blue-black.
➤ A water bath can be set up with a thermometer. Add cold or hot water to regulate the temperature.
➤ Identify the independent, dependent and control variables in the investigation. Write out your method in clear steps.

1. Name two factors that affect the rate of enzyme activity.
2. Describe, in simple terms, how lock and key theory explains enzyme action.
3. State two ways in which bile aids in the digestion of lipids.
4. Which molecules act as building blocks for protein polymers?

Mind map

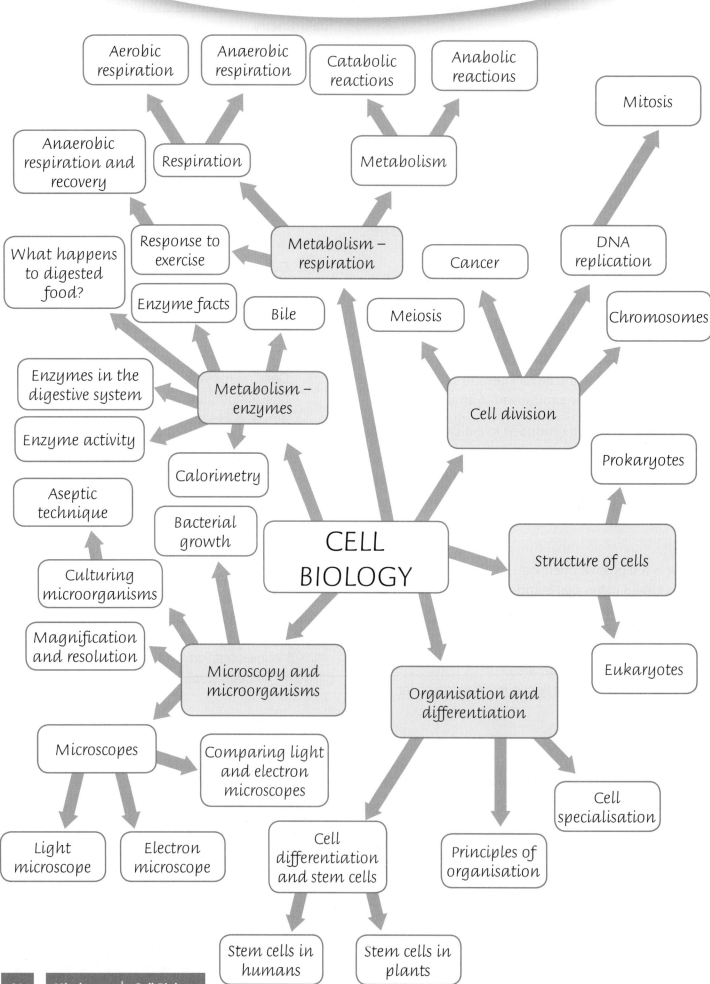

Aerobic respiration

Anaerobic respiration

Catabolic reactions

Anabolic reactions

Mitosis

Anaerobic respiration and recovery

Respiration

Metabolism

DNA replication

What happens to digested food?

Response to exercise

Metabolism – respiration

Cancer

Chromosomes

Enzyme facts

Bile

Meiosis

Enzymes in the digestive system

Metabolism – enzymes

Cell division

Prokaryotes

Enzyme activity

Aseptic technique

Calorimetry

Structure of cells

Magnification and resolution

Bacterial growth

CELL BIOLOGY

Eukaryotes

Culturing microorganisms

Microscopy and microorganisms

Organisation and differentiation

Cell specialisation

Microscopes

Comparing light and electron microscopes

Light microscope

Electron microscope

Cell differentiation and stem cells

Principles of organisation

Stem cells in humans

Stem cells in plants

Practice questions

1. Name the parts of the bacterial cell (**A**–**D**). **(4 marks)**

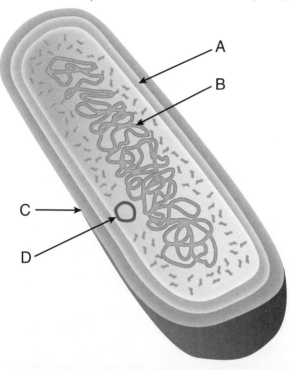

2. Lisa is playing football. She sprints the length of the pitch and scores a goal. However, she can barely celebrate because her legs have gone weak and she is panting heavily.

   a) Explain why Lisa's legs feel weak. **(2 marks)**

   b) Why would Lisa be unable to play the entire game at such a fast pace? **(1 mark)**

   c) Why does aerobic respiration yield more energy from glucose? **(1 mark)**

3. In 1894, the lock and key theory of enzyme action was put forward by Emil Fischer. The diagram shows the first stage in the reaction between an enzyme and a reactant.

   a) What term describes the way that enzyme molecules change at high temperatures? **(1 mark)**

   b) Explain how a drop in pH will affect the structure of the enzyme shown in the diagram. **(2 marks)**

4. Barney has grown some bacterial colonies on an agar plate. He measures the radius of eight colonies. His results are shown in the table below.

Colony	1	2	3	4	5	6	7	8
Radius (mm)	10	8	2	3	2	7	5	4

Using the formula πr^2, calculate the **mean** cross-sectional area of the colonies. **(2 marks)**

Diffusion

Living cells need to obtain oxygen, glucose, water, mineral ions and other dissolved substances from their surroundings. They also need to excrete waste products, such as carbon dioxide or urea. These substances pass through the cell membrane by **diffusion**.

Diffusion:
➤ is the (net) movement of particles in a liquid or gas from a region of high concentration to one of low concentration (down a **concentration gradient**)
➤ happens due to the random motion of particles past each other
➤ stops once the particles have completely spread out
➤ is passive, i.e. requires no input of energy
➤ can be increased in terms of rate by making the concentration gradient steeper, the diffusion path shorter, increasing the temperature or increasing the surface area over which the process occurs, e.g. having a folded cell membrane.

A protist called amoeba can absorb oxygen through diffusion.

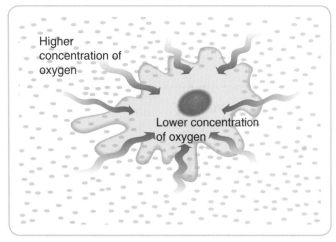

Higher concentration of oxygen

Lower concentration of oxygen

You may be asked to calculate rates of diffusion using **Fick's law**.

$$\text{rate of diffusion} \propto \frac{\text{surface area} \times \text{concentration difference}}{\text{thickness of membrane}}$$

∝ means proportional to

Surface area to volume ratios

A **unicellular organism** (such as a protist) can absorb materials by diffusion directly from the environment. This is because it has a **large** surface area to volume ratio.

However, for a large, **multicellular organism**, the diffusion path between the environment and the inner cells of the body is long. Its large size also means that the **surface area to volume ratio** is **small**.

Adaptations

Multicellular organisms therefore need transport systems and specialised structures for exchanging materials, e.g. mammalian lungs and a small intestine, fish gills, and roots and leaves in plants. These increase diffusion efficiency in animals because they have:
➤ a large surface area
➤ a thin membrane to reduce the diffusion path
➤ an extensive blood supply for transport (animals)
➤ a ventilation system for gaseous exchange, e.g. breathing in animals.

In mammals, the individual air sacs in the lungs increase their surface area by a factor of thousands. Ventilation moves air in and out of the alveoli and the heart moves blood through the capillaries. This maintains the diffusion gradient. The capillary and alveolar linings are very thin, decreasing the diffusion path.

Single alveolus showing how increased surface area enables rapid diffusion of gases

Bunches of alveoli at the end of bronchioles increase surface area

Osmosis

Osmosis is a special case of diffusion that involves the movement of water only. There are two ways of describing osmosis.

1. The net movement of **water** from a region of **low** solute concentration to one of **high** concentration.
2. The movement down a **water potential gradient**.

Osmosis:

➤ occurs across a **partially permeable membrane**, so solute molecules cannot pass through (only water molecules can)
➤ occurs in all organisms
➤ is passive (in other words, requires no input of energy)
➤ allows water movement into root hair cells from the soil and between cells inside the plant
➤ can be demonstrated and measured in plant cells using a variety of tissues, e.g. potato chips, daffodil stems.

Osmosis

| Dilute solution (high concentration of water) | Concentrated solution (low concentration of water) |

Partially permeable membrane

Net movement of water molecules

Active transport

Substances are sometimes absorbed **against** a concentration gradient, i.e. from a low to a high concentration.

Active transport:

➤ requires the release of energy from respiration
➤ takes place in the small intestine in humans, where sugar is absorbed into the bloodstream
➤ occurs via protein carrier molecules in the cell membrane
➤ allows plants to absorb mineral ions from the soil through root hair cells.

A cell absorbing ions by active transport

Root hair cell with high concentration of nitrate ions

Soil with lower concentration of nitrate ions

Cell uses energy to 'pull' ions in against the concentration gradient

(WS) During your course, you may investigate the effect of salt or sugar solutions on plant tissue.

Here is one experiment you could do.
1. Immerse raw potato cut into chips of equal length in sugar solutions of various concentration.
2. You will see the potato chips change in length depending on whether individual cells have lost or gained water.

Can you **predict** what would happen to the potato chips immersed in:
➤ concentrated sugar (e.g. 1 molar)
➤ medium concentration sugar (e.g. 0.5 molar)
➤ water (0 molar)?

Keywords

Surface area to volume ratio ➤ A number calculated by dividing the total surface area of an object by its volume. When the ratio is **high**, the efficiency of diffusion and other processes is **greater**

Water potential/diffusion gradient ➤ A higher concentration of particle numbers in one area than another; in living systems, these areas are often separated by a membrane or cell wall

Partially permeable membrane ➤ A membrane with microscopic holes that allows small particles through (e.g. water) but not large ones (e.g. sugar)

1. Which has the highest surface area to volume ratio – an elephant or a shrew?
2. Some plant tissue is placed in a highly concentrated salt solution. Explain why water leaves the cells.

A plant's system is made up of organs and tissues that enable it to be a **photosynthetic organism**.

These are the main plant structures and their functions.

➤ **Roots** absorb water and minerals. They anchor plants in the soil.

➤ The **stem** transports water and nutrients to leaves. It holds leaves up to the light for maximum absorption of energy.

➤ The **leaf** is the organ of photosynthesis.

➤ The **flower** makes sexual reproduction possible through pollination.

Plant tissues, organs and systems

Leaves

As this cross-section of a leaf shows, leaf tissues are adapted for efficient photosynthesis. The epidermis covers the upper and lower surfaces of the leaf and protects the plant against pathogens.

Upper epidermis – cells are thin and flat to allow light to pass through

Palisade layer (mesophyll) – contains many chloroplasts for light absorption. It is positioned near the top of the leaf to be nearer to sunlight

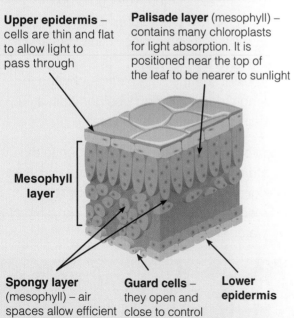

Mesophyll layer

Spongy layer (mesophyll) – air spaces allow efficient diffusion of gases

Guard cells – they open and close to control gas exchange

Lower epidermis

Stem and roots

Veins in the stem, roots and leaves contain tissues that transport water, carbohydrate and minerals around the plant.

➤ **Xylem tissue** transports water and mineral ions from the roots to the rest of the plant.

➤ **Phloem tissue** transports dissolved sugars from the leaves to the rest of the plant.

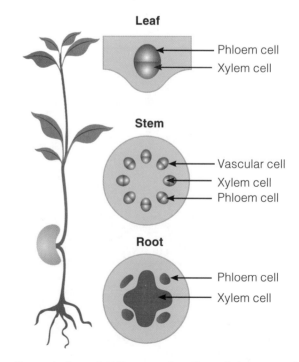

Meristem tissue is found at the growing tips of shoots and roots.

Xylem, phloem and root hair cells

Xylem, phloem and root hair cells are adapted to their function.

Part of plant	Appearance	Function	How they are adapted to their function
Xylem	Hollow tubes made from dead plant cells (the hollow centre is called a lumen)	Transport water and mineral ions from the roots to the rest of the plant in a process called **transpiration**	The cellulose cell walls are thickened and strengthened with a waterproof substance called **lignin**
Phloem	Columns of living cells	**Translocate** (move) cell sap containing sugars (particularly glucose) from the leaves to the rest of the plant, where it is either used or stored	Phloem have pores in the end walls so that the cell sap can move from one phloem cell to the next
Root hair cells	Long and thin; have hair-like extensions	Absorb minerals and water from the soil	Large surface area

Keywords

Photosynthetic organism ➤ Able to absorb light energy and manufacture carbohydrate from carbon dioxide and water

Transpiration ➤ Flow of water through the plant ending in evaporation from leaves

Lignin ➤ Strengthening, waterproof material found in walls of xylem cells

Translocation ➤ Process in which sugars move through the phloem

Xylem Phloem

Xylem   Phloem

➤ If you snap a stick of celery open and pull the two halves apart, long 'strings' will pull away at the break. These are the long vascular tubes that carry water up to the celery's leaves.

➤ Cut a section from a stick of celery and look at it end-on. Can you see the vascular bundles that contain the xylem and phloem? To see the section more clearly, use a hand lens or magnifying glass.

➤ Try putting a celery stick (bottom end down) in a cup of food colouring overnight. When you cut the stem open the next day, you will see the coloured dye in the vascular bundles.

1. What part of the plant organ system allows water to enter the plant?
2. Why are there gaps between cells in the spongy mesophyll?
3. Why do xylem cells not have end walls?

Transport in plants

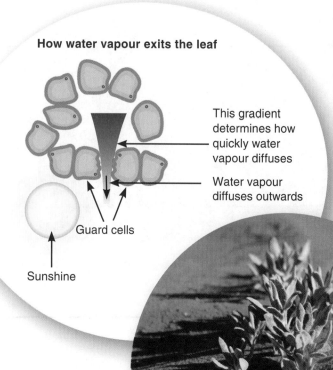

🎧 9

Transpiration

The movement of water through a plant, from roots to leaves, takes place as a transpiration stream. Once water is in the leaves, it diffuses out of the stomata into the surrounding air. This is called **(evapo)transpiration**.

Water evaporates from the spongy mesophyll through the stomata.	Water passes by osmosis from the xylem vessels in the leaf into the spongy mesophyll cells to replace what has been lost.	This movement 'pulls' the column of water in that xylem vessel upwards.	Water enters root hair cells by osmosis to replace water that has entered the xylem.

Measuring rate of transpiration

A potometer

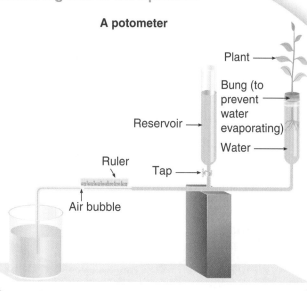

- Plant
- Bung (to prevent water evaporating)
- Reservoir
- Water
- Ruler
- Tap
- Air bubble

A leafy shoot's rate of transpiration can be measured using a **potometer**.

The shoot is held in a tube with a bung around the top to prevent any water from evaporating (this would give a false measurement of the water lost by transpiration).

As the plant transpires, it takes up water from the tube to replace what it has lost. All the water is then pulled up, moving the air bubble along.

The distance the air bubble moves can be used to calculate the plant's rate of transpiration for a given time period.

The experiment can be repeated, varying a different factor each time, to see how each factor affects the rate of transpiration.

Factors affecting rate of transpiration

Evaporation of water from the leaf is affected by **temperature**, **humidity**, **air movement** and **light intensity**.

➤ **Increased temperature** increases the kinetic energy of molecules and removes water vapour more quickly.

➤ **Increased air movement** removes water vapour molecules.

➤ **Increased light intensity** increases the rate of photosynthesis. This in turn draws up more water from the transpiration stream, which maintains high concentration in the spongy mesophyll.

➤ **Decreasing atmospheric humidity** lowers water vapour concentration outside of the stoma and so maintains the concentration gradient.

How water vapour exits the leaf

- This gradient determines how quickly water vapour diffuses
- Water vapour diffuses outwards
- Guard cells
- Sunshine

Opening and closing of stomata

Guard cells control the amount of water vapour that evaporates from the leaves and the amount of carbon dioxide that enters them.

➤ When light intensity is high and photosynthesis is taking place at a rapid rate, the sugar concentration rises in photosynthesising cells, e.g. palisade and guard cells.

➤ Guard cells respond to this by increasing the rate of water movement in the transpiration stream. This in turn provides more water for photosynthesis.

Stomata

Sunshine

High light intensity. Increased photosynthesis rate

More sugar manufactured in guard cells. This raises **solute** concentration in guard cells

Guard cells have increased turgidity, which increases size of stoma allowing more rapid loss of water vapour

Stoma

WS A **hypothesis** is an idea or explanation that you test through study and experiments. It should include a reason. For example: desert plants have fewer stomata than temperate plants **because** they need to minimise water loss.

➤ In an experiment investigating the factors that affect the rate of transpiration, a student plans to take measurements of weight loss or gain from a privet plant.

➤ Construct hypotheses for each of these factors: **temperature**, **humidity**, **air movement** and **light intensity**.

The first has been done for you: As temperature increases, the plant will lose mass/water more quickly **because** diffusion occurs more rapidly.

➤ Paint a thin layer of clear nail varnish onto the underside of a waxy leaf such as laurel – about 2 cm² should be sufficient.

➤ Allow the varnish to dry for at least 15 minutes. This will create a mould of the stomata as the liquid varnish fills the pores in the leaf.

➤ Peel the varnish strip off. Take care not to allow it to fold over or roll.

➤ Prepare it on a microscope slide with a drop of water and a cover slip.

➤ View it under medium power and you should see the stomata.

Compare different types of leaf, e.g. holly and privet, to see which leaves have most stomata. If you don't have a microscope at home, ask to use one at school.

1. What effect would **decreasing** air humidity have on transpiration?
2. In what circumstances might it be beneficial for plants to **close** their stomata?
3. How does water pass from xylem vessels into the leaf?
4. Describe how water passes from roots to leaves.

Keywords

(Evapo)transpiration ➤ Evaporation of water from stomata in the leaf
Turgidity ➤ Where plant cells fill with water and swell as a result of osmosis

Transport in humans 1

Blood circulation

Blood moves around the body in a **double circulatory system**. In other words, blood moves twice through the heart for every full circuit. This ensures maximum efficiency for absorbing oxygen and delivering materials to all living cells.

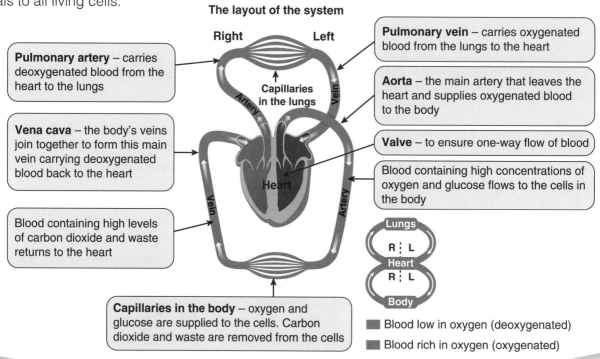

The layout of the system

Right — Left

Pulmonary artery – carries deoxygenated blood from the heart to the lungs

Vena cava – the body's veins join together to form this main vein carrying deoxygenated blood back to the heart

Blood containing high levels of carbon dioxide and waste returns to the heart

Capillaries in the lungs

Artery — Vein

Heart

Vein — Artery

Pulmonary vein – carries oxygenated blood from the lungs to the heart

Aorta – the main artery that leaves the heart and supplies oxygenated blood to the body

Valve – to ensure one-way flow of blood

Blood containing high concentrations of oxygen and glucose flows to the cells in the body

Lungs
R : L
Heart
R : L
Body

Capillaries in the body – oxygen and glucose are supplied to the cells. Carbon dioxide and waste are removed from the cells

▮ Blood low in oxygen (deoxygenated)
▮ Blood rich in oxygen (oxygenated)

The heart

The heart is made of powerful muscles that contract and relax rhythmically in order to continuously pump blood around the body. The **heart muscle** is supplied with food (particularly glucose) and oxygen through the coronary artery.

The sequence of events that takes place when the heart beats is called the **cardiac cycle**.
1. The heart relaxes and blood enters both atria from the veins.
2. The atria contract together to push blood into the ventricles, opening the atrioventricular valves.
3. The ventricles contract from the bottom, pushing blood upwards into the arteries. The backflow of blood into the ventricles is prevented by the **semilunar valves**.

The left side of the heart is more muscular than the right because it has to pump blood further round the body. The right side only has to pump blood to the lungs and back.

A useful measurement for scientists and doctors to take is **cardiac output**. This is calculated using:

cardiac output = stroke volume × heart rate

So, for a person who pumps out 70 ml of blood in one heartbeat (stroke volume) and has a pulse of 70 beats per minute, the cardiac output would be 4900 ml per minute.

Keywords

Coronary artery ➤ The blood vessel delivering blood to the heart muscle

Non-communicable ➤ Disease or condition that cannot be spread from person to person via pathogen transfer

Plaque ➤ Fatty deposits that can build up in arteries

Controlling the heartbeat

The heart is stimulated to beat rhythmically by pacemaker cells. The pacemaker cells produce impulses that spread across the atria to make them contract. Impulses are spread from here down to the ventricles, making them contract, pushing blood up and out.

Pacemaker cells

Nerves connecting the heart to the brain can increase or decrease the pace of the pacemaker cells in order to regulate the heartbeat.

If a person has an irregular heartbeat, they can be fitted with an artificial, electrical pacemaker.

Blood vessels

Blood is carried through the body in three types of vessel.

➤ **Arteries** have thick walls made of elastic fibres and muscle fibres to cope with the high pressure. The **lumen** (space inside) is small compared to the thickness of the walls. There are no valves.

➤ **Veins** have thinner walls. The lumen is much bigger compared to the thickness of the walls and there are valves to prevent the backflow of blood.

➤ **Capillaries** are narrow vessels with walls only one cell thick. These microscopic vessels connect arteries to veins, forming dense networks or **beds**. They are the only blood vessels that have permeable walls to allow the exchange of materials.

Artery

Vein

Valve

Capillary

Note: capillaries are much smaller than veins or arteries

Coronary heart disease

Coronary heart disease (CHD) is a **non-communicable** disease. It results from the build-up of **cholesterol**, leading to plaques laid down in the coronary arteries. This restricts blood flow and the artery may become blocked with a blood clot or **thrombosis**. The heart muscle is deprived of glucose and oxygen, which causes a **heart attack**.

The likelihood of plaque developing increases if you have a high fat diet. The risk of having a heart attack can be reduced by:

➤ eating a balanced diet and not being overweight
➤ not smoking tobacco
➤ lowering alcohol intake
➤ reducing salt levels in your diet
➤ reducing stress levels.

Coronary arteries

Healthy artery

Build-up of fatty material begins

Plaque forms

Plaque ruptures; blood clot forms

1. What is the function of valves in veins?
2. Describe how eating a diet high in fat can lead to a heart attack.

Transport in humans 2

🎧 11

Keywords

Haemoglobin ➤ Iron-containing molecule that binds to oxygen molecules in red blood cells

Ventilation ➤ Process of drawing air into and out of the lungs. It involves the ribs, intercostal muscles and diaphragm

Remedying heart disease

For patients who have heart disease, artificial implants called **stents** can be used to increase blood flow through the coronary artery.

Statins are a type of drug that can be taken to reduce blood cholesterol levels.

In some people, the heart valves may deteriorate, preventing them from opening properly. Alternatively, the valve may develop a leak.

This means that the supply of oxygenated blood to vital organs is reduced. The problem can be corrected by surgical replacement using a **biological** or **mechanical valve**.

When complete heart failure occurs, a heart transplant can be carried out. If a donor heart is unavailable, the patient may be kept alive by an artificial heart until one can be found. Mechanical hearts are also used to give the biological heart a rest while it recovers.

Blood as a tissue

Blood transports digested food and oxygen to cells and removes the cells' waste products. It also forms part of the body's defence mechanism.

The four components of blood are:
➤ platelets
➤ plasma
➤ white blood cells
➤ red blood cells.

Platelets

Tiny cell fragments. They initiate the clotting process and repair damage to blood vessels.

Plasma

A straw-coloured liquid that transports dissolved food materials, urea, carbon dioxide, protein, hormones and antibodies.

White blood cells (phagocytes and lymphocytes)

Protect the body against pathogens. Some have a flexible shape, which enables them to engulf invading microorganisms. Others produce antibodies.

Red blood cells (erythrocytes)

Transport oxygen from lungs to tissues.

Oxygen transport

Red blood cells are small and have a biconcave shape. This gives them a large surface area to volume ratio for absorbing oxygen. When the cells reach the lungs, they absorb and bind to the oxygen in a molecule called **haemoglobin**.

haemoglobin + oxygen $\rightleftharpoons$ oxyhaemoglobin

Blood is then pumped around the body to the tissues, where the reverse of the reaction takes place. Oxygen diffuses out of the red blood cells and into the tissues.

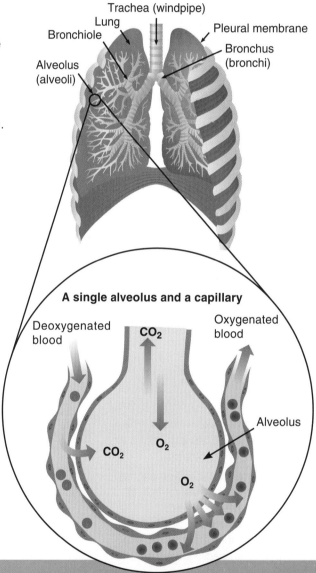

Transport of oxygen in red blood cells

Oxygen from alveolus — Red blood cell

Haemoglobin molecules

Oxygen released to cells

The lungs

Humans, like many vertebrates, have lungs to act as a **gaseous exchange surface**.

Other structures in the **thorax** enable air to enter and leave the lungs (**ventilation**).

➤ The **trachea** is a flexible tube, surrounded by rings of cartilage to stop it collapsing. Air is breathed in via the mouth and passes through here on its way to the lungs.
➤ **Bronchi** are branches of the trachea.
➤ The **alveoli** are small air sacs that provide a large surface area for the exchange of gases.
➤ **Capillaries** form a dense network to absorb maximum oxygen and release carbon dioxide.

In the alveoli, **oxygen** diffuses down a concentration gradient. It moves across the thin layers of cells in the alveolar and capillary walls, and into the red blood cells.

For **carbon dioxide**, the gradient operates in reverse. The carbon dioxide passes from the blood to the alveoli, and from there it travels back up the air passages to the mouth.

The lungs

Trachea (windpipe)
Lung
Bronchiole
Alveolus (alveoli)
Pleural membrane
Bronchus (bronchi)

A single alveolus and a capillary

Deoxygenated blood
CO_2
Oxygenated blood
CO_2
O_2
Alveolus
O_2

WS Scientists make observations, take measurements and gather data using a variety of instruments and techniques. Recording data is an important skill.

Create a table template that you could use to record data for the following experiment:

An investigation that involves measuring the resting and active pulse rates of 30 boys and 30 girls, together with their average breathing rates.

Make sure that:
➤ you have the correct number of columns and rows
➤ each variable is in a heading
➤ units are in the headings (so they don't need to be repeated in the body of the table).

1. What are the differences between lymphocytes and red blood cells?
2. Describe the route that would be travelled by a molecule of oxygen through the body until it reached a respiring muscle cell. State the cells, tissue, organs and processes that are involved.

Photosynthesis

Plants are **producers**. This means they can photosynthesise, i.e. make food molecules in the form of **carbohydrate** from the simple molecules, carbon dioxide and water. As such, they are the main producers of **biomass**. Sunlight energy is needed for photosynthesis.

Photosynthesis:
- is an **endothermic** reaction
- requires **chlorophyll** to absorb the sunlight; this is found in the **chloroplasts** of photosynthesising cells, e.g. palisade cells, guard cells and spongy mesophyll cells
- produces **glucose**, which is then respired for energy release or converted to other useful molecules for the plant
- produces **oxygen** that has built up in the atmosphere over millions of years; oxygen is vital for respiration in all organisms.

carbon dioxide + water $\xrightarrow[\text{chlorophyll}]{\text{light energy}}$ glucose + oxygen

HT $6CO_2 + 6H_2O \xrightarrow[\text{chlorophyll}]{\text{light energy}} C_6H_{12}O_6 + 6O_2$

Rate of photosynthesis
The rate of photosynthesis can be affected by:
- temperature
- light intensity
- carbon dioxide concentration
- amount of chlorophyll.

In a given set of circumstances, **temperature**, **light intensity** and **carbon dioxide concentration** can act as **limiting factors**.

Temperature	Light intensity	Carbon dioxide concentration
① As the temperature rises, so does the rate of photosynthesis. This means temperature is limiting the rate of photosynthesis.	① As the light intensity increases, so does the rate of photosynthesis. This means light intensity is limiting the rate of photosynthesis.	① As carbon dioxide concentration increases, so does the rate of photosynthesis. Carbon dioxide concentration is the limiting factor.
② As the temperature approaches 45°C, the enzymes controlling photosynthesis start to be denatured. The rate of photosynthesis decreases and eventually declines to zero.	② Eventually, the rise in light intensity has no effect on photosynthesis rate. Light intensity is no longer the limiting factor; carbon dioxide or temperature must be.	② Eventually, the rise in carbon dioxide concentration has no effect – it is no longer the limiting factor.

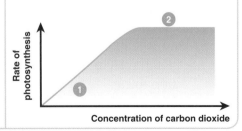

You need to understand that each factor has the potential to increase the rate of photosynthesis.

(HT) You also need to explain how these factors interact in terms of which variable is acting as the limiting factor.

The inverse law

The effect of light intensity on photosynthesis can be investigated by placing a lamp at varying distances from a plant. As the lamp is moved further away from the plant the light intensity decreases, as shown in the graph.

Distance from plant

There is an **inverse relationship** between the two variables. The graph can be used to convert distances to light intensity, or light intensity can be calculated using the formula:

$$\text{light intensity} = \frac{1}{d^2}$$
> *d* is the distance from the lamp.

There are no units of light intensity – it has an arbitrary scale.

Commercial applications

Farmers and market gardeners can increase their crop yields in greenhouses. They do this by:
➤ making the temperature optimum for growth using heaters
➤ increasing light intensity using lamps
➤ installing fossil-fuel burning stoves to increase carbon dioxide concentration (and increase temperature).

If applied carefully, the cost of adding these features will be offset by increased profit from the resulting crop.

Keywords

Biomass ➤ Mass of organisms calculated by multiplying their individual mass by the number that exist

Endothermic ➤ A change that requires the input of energy

Chlorophyll ➤ A molecule that gives plants their green colour and absorbs light energy

Limiting factor ➤ A variable that, if changed, will influence the rate of reaction most

Cellulose ➤ Large carbohydrate molecule found in all plants; an essential constituent of cell walls

Uses of glucose in plants

The glucose produced from photosynthesis can be used immediately in respiration, but some is used to synthesise larger molecules: **starch**, **cellulose**, **protein** and **lipids**.

Starch is insoluble. So it is suitable for storage in leaves, stem or roots.

Cellulose is needed for cell walls.

Protein is used for the growth and repair of plant tissue, and also to synthesise enzyme molecules.

Lipids are needed in cell membranes, and for fat and oil storage in seeds.

Use plasticine and coloured paper / card to produce a molecular model showing the photosynthesis reaction. Use ideas from the 'Uses of glucose in plants' section to help you.

🎧12 ☑

1. Give two reasons why photosynthesis is seen as the opposite of respiration.
(HT) 2. What **economic** factor must market gardeners consider before installing wood-burning stoves in their greenhouses?

Mind map

Adaptations

Surface to area volume ratios

Diffusion

Osmosis

Remedying heart disease

Blood as a tissue

Cell transport

Leaves

Active transport

Transport in humans 2

Plant tissues, organs and systems

Oxygen transport

The lungs

TRANSPORT SYSTEMS

Stem and roots

Coronary heart disease

Transport in plants

Xylem, phloem and root hair cells

Blood vessels

Transport in humans 1

Transpiration

The heart

Controlling the heartbeat

Blood circulation

Opening and closing of stomata

Factors affecting rate of transpiration

The inverse law

Commercial applications

PHOTOSYNTHESIS

Rate of photosynthesis

Uses of glucose in plants

Practice questions

1. Which of the following are examples of osmosis? Tick (✓) the three correct options. **(3 marks)**

   a) Water evaporating from leaves ☐

   b) Water moving from plant cell to plant cell and back again ☐

   c) Mixing pure water and sugar solution ☐

   d) A pear submerged in a concentrated sugar solution losing water ☐

   e) Water moving from blood plasma to body cells ☐

   f) Sugar being absorbed from the intestine into the blood ☐

2. Emphysema is a lung disease that increases the thickness of the surface of the lungs for gas exchange and reduces the total area available for gas exchange.

   Two men did the same amount of exercise. One man was in good health and the other man had emphysema.

   The results are shown in the table.

	Healthy man	Man with emphysema
Total air flowing into lungs (dm³/min)	89.5	38.9
Oxygen entering blood (dm³/min)	2.5	1.2

   a) Which man had more oxygen entering his blood? **(1 mark)**

   b) Explain why the man with emphysema struggled to carry out exercise. **(2 marks)**

3. The diagram shows two types of blood vessel.

   A B

   a) Name each type of blood vessel. **(2 marks)**

   b) Explain why blood vessel A has a thick, elastic muscle wall. **(1 mark)**

   c) Why does blood vessel B have valves? **(1 mark)**

Non-communicable diseases

Keywords

Pathogen ➤ A microorganism that causes disease

Symptoms ➤ Physical or mental features that indicate a condition or disease, e.g. rash, high temperature, vomiting

Immune system ➤ A system of cells and other components that protect the body from pathogens and other foreign substances

Malnutrition ➤ A diet lacking in one or more food groups

13

Communicable diseases are caused by **pathogens** such as bacteria and viruses. They can be transmitted from organism to organism in a variety of ways. Examples include cholera and tuberculosis.

Non-communicable diseases are not primarily caused by pathogens. Examples are diseases caused by a poor diet, diabetes, heart disease and smoking-related diseases.

Health is the state of physical, social and mental well-being. Many factors can have an effect on health, including stress and life situations.

Risk factors

Non-communicable diseases often result from a combination of several **risk factors**.

➤ Risk factors produce an increased likelihood of developing that particular disease. They can be aspects of a person's lifestyle or substances found in the body or environment.

➤ Some of these factors are difficult to quantify or to establish as a definite **causal connection**. So scientists have to describe their effects in terms of probability or likelihood.

The **symptoms** observed in the body may result from communicable and non-communicable components interacting.

A lowered **immune system** may make a person more vulnerable to infection.

Immune reactions caused by pathogens can trigger allergies such as asthma and skin rashes.

Symptoms

Viruses inhabiting living cells can change them into cancer cells.

Serious physical health problems can lead to **mental illness** such as depression.

Poor diet

People need a **balanced diet**.

If a diet does not include enough of the main food groups, **malnutrition** might result. Lack of correct vitamins leads to diseases such as **scurvy** and **rickets**. Lack of the mineral, iron, results in **anaemia**.

A high fat diet contributes to cardiovascular disease and high levels of salt increase blood pressure.

Smoking tobacco

Chemicals in tobacco smoke affect health.

➤ **Carbon monoxide** decreases the blood's oxygen-carrying capacity.

➤ **Nicotine** raises the heart rate and therefore blood pressure.

➤ **Tar** triggers cancer.

➤ **Particulates** cause **emphysema** and increase the likelihood of **lung infections**.

Weight/lack of exercise

Obesity and lack of exercise both increase the risk of developing **type 2 diabetes** and cardiovascular disease.

One way to show whether someone is underweight or overweight for their height is to calculate their **body mass index (BMI)**, using the following formula:

$$BMI = \frac{mass\ (kg)}{height^2\ (m)}$$

Recommended BMI chart

BMI	What it means
<18.5	Underweight – too light for your height
18.5–25	Ideal – correct weight range for your height
25–30	Overweight – too heavy
30–40	Obese – much too heavy. Health risks!

Example:
Calculate a man's BMI if he is 1.65 m tall and weighs 68 kg.

$$BMI = \frac{mass\ (kg)}{height^2\ (m)} = \frac{68}{1.65^2} = \frac{68}{2.7} = 25$$

The recommended BMI for his height (1.65 m) is 18.5–25, so he is just a healthy weight.

There are drawbacks to using BMI as a way of assessing people's health. For example:

➤ teenagers go through a rapid growth phase
➤ a person could have a well-developed muscle system – this would increase their body mass but not make them obese.

Some scientists say a more accurate method is using the waist/hip ratio. A tape measure is used to measure the circumference of the hips and the waist (at its widest). The following chart can then be used.

Waist to hip ratio (WHR)		
Male	Female	Health risk based solely on WHR
0.95 or below	0.80 or below	Low
0.96 to 1.0	0.81 to 0.85	Moderate
1.0+	0.85+	High

Alcohol
Drinking excess alcohol can impair brain function and lead to **cirrhosis** of the liver. It also contributes to some types of cancer and cardiovascular disease.

Smoking and drinking alcohol during pregnancy
Unborn babies receive nutrition from the mother via the placenta. Substances from tobacco, alcohol and other drugs can pass to the baby and cause **lower birth weight**, **foetal alcohol syndrome** and **addiction**.

Carcinogens
Exposure to **ionising radiation** (for example, X-rays, gamma rays) can cause cancerous tumours. Overexposure to UV light can cause skin cancer. Certain chemicals such as mercury can also increase the likelihood of cancer.

(WS) Interpreting complex data in graphs doesn't need to be difficult. This line graph shows data about smoking and lung cancer. Look for different patterns in it. For example:

➤ males have higher smoking rates in all years
➤ female cancer rates have increased overall since 1972.

Can you see any other patterns?

Smoking habits and lung cancer incidence in a European country

KEY
✖✖✖ Male smoking data — Male incidence of lung cancer
●—●—● Female smoking data - - - Female incidence of lung cancer

1. State three factors that cause cancer.
2. Give one consequence of a lowered immune system.

Communicable diseases

How do pathogens spread?

Pathogens are disease-causing microorganisms from groups of bacteria, viruses, fungi and protists. All animals and plants can be affected by pathogens. They spread in many ways, including:

➤ **droplet infection** (sneezing and coughing), e.g. flu

➤ **physical contact**, such as touching a contaminated object or person, e.g. Ebola virus

➤ **transmission** by transferral of or contact **with bodily fluids**, e.g. hepatitis B

➤ **sexual transmission**, e.g. HIV, gonorrhoea

➤ **contamination of food or water**, e.g. Salmonella, cholera

➤ **animal bites**, e.g. rabies.

How do pathogens cause harm?

➤ Bacteria and viruses reproduce rapidly in the body.

➤ Viruses cause cell damage.

➤ Bacteria produce toxins that damage tissues.

These effects produce **symptoms** in the body.

How can the spread of disease be prevented?

The spread of disease can be prevented by:

➤ good hygiene, e.g. washing hands/whole body, using soaps and disinfectants

➤ destroying **vectors**, e.g. disrupting the life cycle of mosquitoes can combat malaria

➤ the isolation or quarantine of individuals

➤ vaccination.

Bacterial diseases

Disease	Transmission	Symptoms	Treatment/prevention
Tuberculosis	Droplet infection	Persistent coughing, which may bring up blood; chest pain; weight loss; fatigue; fever; night sweats; chills	Long course of antibiotics
Cholera	Contaminated water/food	Diarrhoea; vomiting; dehydration	Rehydration salts
Chlamydia	Sexually transmitted	May not be present, but can include discharge and bleeding from sex organs	Antibiotics Using condoms during sexual intercourse can reduce chances of infection
Helicobacter	Spread orally from person to person by saliva, or by fecal contamination	Abdominal pain; feeling bloated; nausea; vomiting; loss of appetite; weight loss	Proton pump inhibitors and antibiotics
Salmonella	Contaminated food containing toxins from pathogens – these could be introduced from unhygienic food preparation techniques	Vomiting; fever; diarrhoea, stomach cramps	Anti-diarrhoeals and antibiotics; vaccinations for chickens
Gonorrhoea	Sexually transmitted	Thick yellow or green discharge from vagina or penis; pain on urination	Antibiotic injection followed by antibiotic tablets; penicillin is no longer effective against gonorrhoea; prevention through use of condoms

Fungal diseases

Disease	Transmission	Symptoms	Treatment/prevention
Athlete's foot	Direct and indirect contact, e.g. skin-to-skin, bed sheets and towels (often spreads at swimming pools and in changing rooms)	Itchy, red, scaly, flaky and dry skin	Self-care and anti-fungal medication externally applied

Viral and protist diseases

Disease	Transmission	Symptoms and notes	Treatment/prevention
Measles (viral)	Droplets from sneezes and coughs	Fever; red skin rash; fatal if complications arise	No specific treatment; vaccine is a highly effective preventative measure
HIV (viral)	Sexually transmitted; exchange of body fluids; sharing of needles during drug use	Flu-like symptoms initially; late-stage AIDS produces complications due to compromised immune system	Anti-retroviral drugs
Ebola (viral)	Via body fluids; contaminated needles; bite from infected animal	Early stages: muscle pain; sore throat; diarrhoea Later stages: kidney/liver failure; internal bleeding	No direct treatments or tested vaccines are available at the time of writing; symptoms and infections are treated as they appear
Malaria (protist)	Via mosquito vector	Headache; sweats; chills and vomiting; symptoms disappear and reappear on a cyclical basis; further life-threatening complications may arise	Various anti-malarial drugs are available for both prevention and cure; prevention of mosquito breeding and use of mosquito nets

Viruses carry out their life cycle largely within a host cell. Viruses tend to follow one of two types of cycle.

➤ **Lysogenic**: the virus does not lyse (split) the host cell. Instead, the viral DNA becomes part of the host DNA. When the host cell divides, the viral DNA is also copied and is present in each of the daughter cells.

➤ **Lytic**: the virus replicates using the host DNA (as before). The new viruses that are formed destroy the infected cell and its membrane as they are released.

Influenza viral life cycle

Binding to the target cell

Budding

Replication

Viral protein synthesis

New virion

➤ Create cards showing information about the disease-causing microorganisms in this module. Each card should have the name of the disease at the top and then list the symptoms, mode of transmission, etc.

➤ Use the cards with a revision buddy. You could give a score for each category of information, e.g. contagion factor (how easily the disease is transmitted), severity of symptoms, etc.

Keywords

Droplet infection ➤ Transmission of microorganisms through the aerosol (water droplets) produced through coughing and sneezing

Vectors ➤ Small organisms (such as mosquitoes or ticks) that pass on pathogens between people or places

1. Why is cholera transmitted rapidly in areas that have poor sanitation (sewage systems)?
2. Name two diseases that cause a rash or affect the skin in some way.

Human defences

Keywords

Epithelial ➤ A single layer of cells often found lining respiratory and digestive structures

Mucus ➤ Thick fluid produced in the lining of respiratory and digestive passages

Cilia ➤ Microscopic hairs found on the surface of epithelial cells; they 'waft' from side to side in a rhythmic manner

Antigen ➤ Molecular marker on a pathogen cell membrane that acts as a recognition point for antibodies

Antibodies ➤ Proteins produced by white blood cells (particularly lymphocytes). They lock on to antigens and neutralise them

Immunological memory ➤ The system of cells and cell products whose function is to prevent and destroy microbial infection

Non-specific defences

The body has a number of general or non-specific defences to stop pathogens multiplying inside it.

The skin covers most of the body – it is a **physical barrier** to pathogens. It also secretes antimicrobial peptides to kill microorganisms. If the skin is damaged, a clotting mechanism takes place in the blood preventing pathogens from entering the site of the wound.

Tears contain enzymes called **lysozymes**. Lysozymes break down pathogen cells that might otherwise gain entry to the body through tear ducts.

Hairs in the **nose** trap particles that may contain pathogens.

Tubes in the respiratory system (**trachea** and **bronchi**) are lined with special **epithelial** cells. These cells either produce a sticky, liquid **mucus** that traps microorganisms or have tiny hairs called **cilia** that move the mucus up to the mouth where it is swallowed.

The **stomach** produces **hydrochloric acid**, which kills microorganisms.

Skin

Tears

Nose

Epithelial cells

Cilia

Mucus produced here

Stomach

Phagocytes are a type of **white blood cell**. They move around in the bloodstream and body tissues searching for pathogens. When they find pathogens, they **engulf** and digest them in a process called **phagocytosis**.

White blood cell (phagocyte)

| Microorganisms invade the body | The white blood cell surrounds and ingests the microorganisms | The white blood cell starts to digest the microorganisms | The microorganisms have been digested by the white blood cell |

Specific defences

White blood cells called **lymphocytes** recognise molecular markers on pathogens called **antigens**. They produce **antibodies** that lock on to the antigens on the cell surface of the pathogen cell. The immobilised cells are clumped together and engulfed by phagocytes.

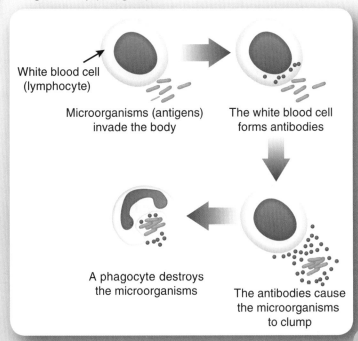

White blood cell (lymphocyte)

Microorganisms (antigens) invade the body

The white blood cell forms antibodies

A phagocyte destroys the microorganisms

The antibodies cause the microorganisms to clump

Some white blood cells produce **antitoxins** that neutralise the poisons produced from some pathogens.

Every pathogen has its own unique antigens. Lymphocytes make antibodies specifically for a particular antigen.

Example: Antibodies to fight TB will not fight cholera

TB microorganism

Antibodies

Antigens

White blood cells

Cholera microorganism

Antibodies binding to virus

Active immunity

Once lymphocytes recognise a particular pathogen, the interaction is stored as part of the body's **immunological memory** through **memory lymphocytes**. These memory cells can produce the right antibodies much quicker if the same pathogen is detected again, therefore providing future protection against the disease. The process is called the **secondary response** and is part of the body's **active immunity**. Active immunity can also be achieved through vaccination.

Memory lymphocytes and antibody production

2nd exposure to pathogen

1st exposure to pathogen

Antibody level

Time

(WS) Investigating the growth of pathogens in the laboratory involves culturing microorganisms (see Module 3). This presents hazards that require a **risk assessment**. A risk assessment involves taking into account the severity of each hazard and the likelihood that it will occur.

Any experiment of this type involves thinking about risks in advance. Here is an example of a risk assessment table for this investigation.

Hazard	Infection from pathogen	Scald from autoclave (a specialised pressure cooker for superheating its contents)
Risk	High	High
How to lower the risk	➤ Observe **aseptic technique**. ➤ Wash hands thoroughly before and after experiment. ➤ Store plates at a maximum temperature of 25°C.	➤ Ensure lid is tightly secured. ➤ Adjust heat to prevent too high a pressure. ➤ Wait for autoclave to cool down before removing lid.

1. Describe the process of phagocytosis.
2. Explain how active immunity can be developed in the body.

Fighting disease

Keywords

Sensitisation ➤ Cells in the immune system are able to 'recognise' antigens or foreign cells and respond by attacking them or producing antibodies

Herd immunity ➤ Vaccination of a significant portion of a population (or herd) makes it hard for a disease to spread because there are so few people left to infect. This gives protection to susceptible individuals such as the elderly or infants

Inhibition ➤ The effect of one agent against another in order to slow down or stop activity, e.g. chemical reactions can be slowed down using inhibitors. Some hormones are inhibitors

Vaccination
There are two types of vaccination.

Passive immunisation
Antibodies are introduced into an individual's body, rather than the person producing them on their own. Some pathogens or toxins (e.g. snake venom) act very quickly and a person's immune system cannot produce antibodies quickly enough. So the person must be injected with the antibodies. However, this does not give long-term protection.

Active immunisation

First vaccination

Booster vaccination a few weeks later

Rapid production of antibodies should the pathogen invade the body

Protective level

y-axis: Level of antibody
x-axis: Time (months) — 0, 2, 4, 6, 8

Immunisation gives a person immunity to a disease without the pathogens multiplying in the body, or the person having symptoms.

1. A weakened or inactive strain of the pathogen is injected. The pathogen is heat-treated so it cannot multiply. The antigen molecules remain intact.

2. Even though they are harmless, the antigens on the pathogen trigger the white blood cells to produce specific antibodies.

3. As with natural immunity, **memory lymphocytes** remain **sensitised**. This means they can produce more antibodies very quickly if the same pathogen is detected again.

HT

Benefits of immunisation	Risks of immunisation
➤ It protects against diseases that could kill or cause disability (e.g. polio, measles).	➤ A person could have an allergic reaction to the vaccine (small risk).
➤ If everybody is vaccinated and **herd immunity** is established, the disease eventually dies out (this is what happened to smallpox).	

Influenza Vaccine

10 ml

Antibiotics and painkillers

Diseases caused by bacteria (not viruses) can be treated using **antibiotics**, e.g. penicillin. Antibiotics are drugs that destroy the pathogen. Some bacteria need to be treated with antibiotics specific to them.

Antibiotics work because they **inhibit** cell processes in the bacteria but not the body of the host.

Viral diseases can be treated with **antiviral drugs**, e.g. swine flu can be treated with 'Tamiflu' tablets. It is a challenge to develop drugs that destroy viruses without harming body tissues.

Antibiotic resistance

Antibiotics are very effective at killing bacteria. However, some bacteria are **naturally resistant** to particular antibiotics. It is important for patients to follow instructions carefully and take the full course of antibiotics so that all the harmful bacteria are killed.

If doctors over-prescribe antibiotics, there is more chance of resistant bacteria surviving. These multiply and spread, making the antibiotic useless. **MRSA** is a bacterium that has become resistant to most antibiotics. These bacteria have been called 'superbugs'.

Painkillers

Painkillers or **analgesics** are given to patients to relieve symptoms of a disease, but they do not kill pathogens. Types of painkiller include paracetamol and ibuprofen. Morphine is another painkiller – it is a medicinal form of heroin used to treat extreme pain.

The effect of antibiotics on infection

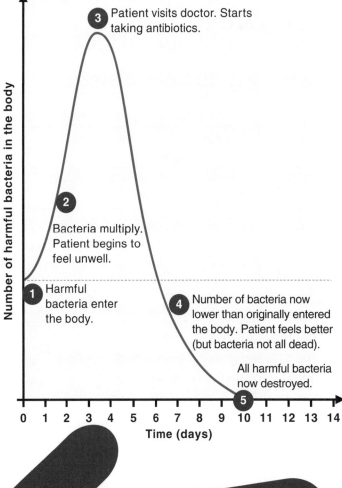

Number of harmful bacteria in the body → Time (days)

3 Patient visits doctor. Starts taking antibiotics.

2 Bacteria multiply. Patient begins to feel unwell.

1 Harmful bacteria enter the body.

4 Number of bacteria now lower than originally entered the body. Patient feels better (but bacteria not all dead).

5 All harmful bacteria now destroyed.

0 1 2 3 4 5 6 7 8 9 10 11 12 13 14

If you are revising with friends, try doing a role-play. This will help you visualise the actions of cells and processes in the immune system.
Plan and rehearse a scenario where a pathogen enters the human body and multiplies.

▶ Allocate roles for the pathogens and the various immune components: phagocytes, lymphocytes, antibodies, etc. You could even have a narrator.

▶ Mimic the actions of the various cells. How could you do this effectively?

▶ Ask someone to watch the role-play and give you feedback on what went well and what you could improve.

1. What is the difference between an antibiotic and an antibody?
2. What is the difference between an antiviral and an analgesic?
3. What can doctors and patients do to reduce the risk of antibiotic-resistant bacteria developing?

Drugs used for treating illnesses and health conditions include antibiotics, analgesics and other chemicals that modify body processes and chemical reactions. In the past, these drugs were obtained from plants and microorganisms.

Discovery and development of drugs

17

Discovery of drugs

The following drugs are obtained from plants and microorganisms.

Name of drug	Where it is found/origin	Use
Digitalis	Foxgloves (common garden plants that are found in the wild)	Slows down the heartbeat; can be used to treat heart conditions
Aspirin	Willow trees (aspirin contains the **active ingredient** salicylic acid)	Mild painkiller
Penicillin	Penicillium mould (discovered by Alexander Fleming)	Antibiotic

Modern **pharmaceutical drugs** are synthesised by chemists in laboratories, usually at great cost. The starting point might still be a chemical extracted from a plant.

New drugs have to be developed all the time to combat new and different diseases. This is a lengthy process, taking up to ten years. During this time the drugs are tested to determine:

➤ that they work
➤ that they are safe
➤ that they are given at the correct **dose** (early tests usually involve low doses).

New drugs made in laboratory ➡ Drugs tested in laboratory for toxicity using cells, tissues and live animals ➡ Clinical trials involving healthy volunteers and patients to check for side-effects

In addition to testing, **computer models** are used to predict how the drug will affect cells, based on knowledge about how the body works and the effects of similar drugs. There are many who believe this type of testing should be extended and that animal testing should be phased out.

Clinical trials

Clinical trials are carried out on healthy volunteers and patients who have the disease. Some are given the new drug and others are given a **placebo**. The effects of the drug can then be compared to the effects of taking the placebo.

Blind trials involve volunteers who do not know if they have been given the new drug or a placebo. This eliminates any psychological factors and helps to provide a fair comparison. (Blind trials are not normally used in modern clinical trials.)

Double blind trials involve volunteers who are randomly allocated to groups. **Neither they nor the doctors/scientists** know if they have been given the new drug or a placebo. This eliminates **all** bias from the test.

New drugs must also be tested against the best existing treatments.

Keywords

Active ingredient ➤ Chemical in a drug that has a therapeutic effect (other chemicals in the drug simply enhance flavour or act as bulking agents)
Pharmaceutical drug ➤ Chemicals that are developed artificially and taken by a patient to relieve symptoms of a disease or treat a condition
Placebo ➤ A substitute for the medication that does not contain the active ingredient
HT **Hybridoma cells** ➤ Cells produced by the fusion of lymphocytes and a tumour cell

WS When studies involving new drugs are published, there is a **peer review**. This is where scientists with appropriate knowledge read the scientific study and examine the data to see if it is **valid**. Sometimes the trials are duplicated by others to see if similar results are obtained. This increases the **reliability** of the findings and filters out false or exaggerated claims.

Once a **consensus** is agreed, the paper is published. This allows others to hear about the work and to develop it further.

In the case of pharmaceutical drugs, clinical bodies have to decide if the drug can be **licensed** (allowed to be used) and whether it is **cost-effective**. This can be controversial because a potentially life-saving drug may not be used widely simply because it costs too much and/or would benefit too few people.

HT Monoclonal antibodies

Monoclonal antibodies are used to treat diseases and in technological applications. They are artificially produced in the laboratory.

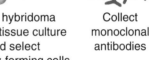

Tumour cells (myeloma)

Vaccinate mouse to stimulate the production of antibodies

Collect spleen cells that form antibodies from mouse

Spleen cells are a type of lymphocyte and can't reproduce on their own, so they fuse (join) with myeloma cells to form hybridoma cells

Grow hybridoma cells in tissue culture and select antibody-forming cells

Collect monoclonal antibodies

The **hybridoma cells** are important because they divide rapidly (by cloning) and produce the required antibody. This means that millions of identical cloned cells are made, which can then be **purified** and used.

Uses of monoclonal antibodies

Use	How?	Advantages
Cancer treatment	Antibodies are made that react to an antigen found on a cancer cell, e.g. in a pancreatic cancer tumour. A toxic agent, such as a radioactive substance, is bound to the antibody and can then be injected into the patient.	The antibody enables the agent to be carried directly to cancer cells and does not harm other cells in the body (unlike chemotherapy and radiotherapy). The technique can also be used to locate blood clots.
Pregnancy testing kits	HCG is a hormone produced in pregnancy. Antibodies to the protein hormone are bound to a test strip and used to detect HCG in urine.	Rapid results (within minutes).
Measuring hormone levels in laboratories	Antibodies can be used to detect hormones or to detect pathogens and other chemicals in the blood.	Provides new information that wouldn't otherwise have been available.
Research	Used to locate a specific molecule in cells or tissues by binding to them with a fluorescent marker.	Marking of molecules made more specific.

When using monoclonal antibodies to treat cancer, more side-effects than expected can arise.

1. What are the alternatives to testing drugs on animals?

HT 2. List two uses of monoclonal antibodies.

Plant diseases

Keywords

HT Diagnostic ➤ A process used to identify or recognise a disease or pathogen

Chlorosis ➤ Where leaves lose their colour as a result of mineral deficiency

HT Detecting and identifying plant diseases

Plant diseases and pests cause widespread damage to plants in the wild and in agriculture. They threaten food stocks, affect ecosystems and cause a loss to the economy.

Identifying and detecting plant diseases involves several stages.

Look for:
➤ stunted growth
➤ leaf spots
➤ areas of decay
➤ growths/tumours
➤ malformed stems and leaves
➤ discolouration
➤ presence of pests.

➤ Eliminate environmental causes, e.g. abrasion, poor water supply, climatic factors.

➤ Study the distribution of affected plants and refer to garden manuals or websites.

➤ Carry out **diagnostic** testing in a laboratory to identify pathogens, e.g. observation; using monoclonal antibody testing kits; DNA testing.

Pathogens and pests that affect plants

Disease	Pathogen	Appearance/effect on plants	Treatment
Rose black spot	Fungal disease – the fungal spores are spread by water and wind	Purple/black spots on leaves; these then turn yellow and drop early, leading to a lack of photosynthesis and poor growth	Apply a fungicide and/or remove affected leaves
Tobacco mosaic virus (TMV)	Widespread disease that affects many plants (including tomatoes)	'Mosaic' pattern of discolouration; can lead to lack of photosynthesis and poor growth	
Ash dieback	Caused by the fungus *Chalara*	Leaf loss and bark lesions	Cut back or remove diseased trees to reduce chance of airborne spores
Barley powdery mildew	*Erysiphe graminis*	Causes powdery mildew to appear on grasses, including cereals	Fungicides and careful application of nitrogen fertilisers
Crown gall disease	*Agrobacterium tumefaciens*	Tumours or 'galls' at the crown of plants such as apple, raspberry and rose	Use of copper and methods of biological control

Pests	What they do	Appearance/effect on plants	Control
Invertebrates and particularly insects, e.g. many species of aphids	Feed on sap, leaves and storage organs; transmit pathogenic viruses		Chemical pesticides or biological control methods

Mineral ion deficiencies

Plants need **mineral ions** to build complex molecules. The ions are obtained from the soil via the roots in an active manner (requiring energy). In particular, plants need:

➤ **nitrates** to form **amino acids**, the building blocks of **proteins**. They are also needed to make nucleic acids such as **DNA**. Lack of nitrates in a plant leads to yellow leaves and stunted growth

➤ **magnesium** to form chlorophyll, which absorbs light energy for photosynthesis. Lack of magnesium results in **chlorosis**, which is a discolouration of the leaves.

Defence responses of plants

Plants defend themselves from herbivores and disease in a range of ways. These adaptations have evolved over millions of years to maximise a plant's survival.

Mechanical defences include:

➤ thorns and hairs to deter plant-eaters
➤ leaves that droop or curl on contact
➤ mimicry, to fool animals into avoiding them as food or laying their eggs on them. For example, passion flowers have structures that look like yellow eggs. A butterfly is less likely to lay eggs on a plant that has apparently already been used.

Physical defences include:

➤ tough, waxy leaf cuticles
➤ cellulose cell walls
➤ layers of dead cells around stems, e.g. bark. These fall off, taking pathogens with them.

Chemical defences include:

➤ producing antibacterial chemicals, e.g. mint and witch hazel
➤ producing toxins to deter herbivores, e.g. deadly nightshade, foxgloves and tobacco plants.

Revise and test yourself on this topic by designing a set of question/answer cards.

➤ Each card should look like a domino with two halves.
➤ On one side, write a question. On the other, write the answer to a question from the next card. The last card's answer should loop back to the first card's question.
➤ Then shuffle and re-organise the cards and start playing!

1. List three things that plant scientists look for when detecting whether a plant is diseased.
2. Why is the tobacco mosaic virus so damaging to plants?

🎧 18

Mind map

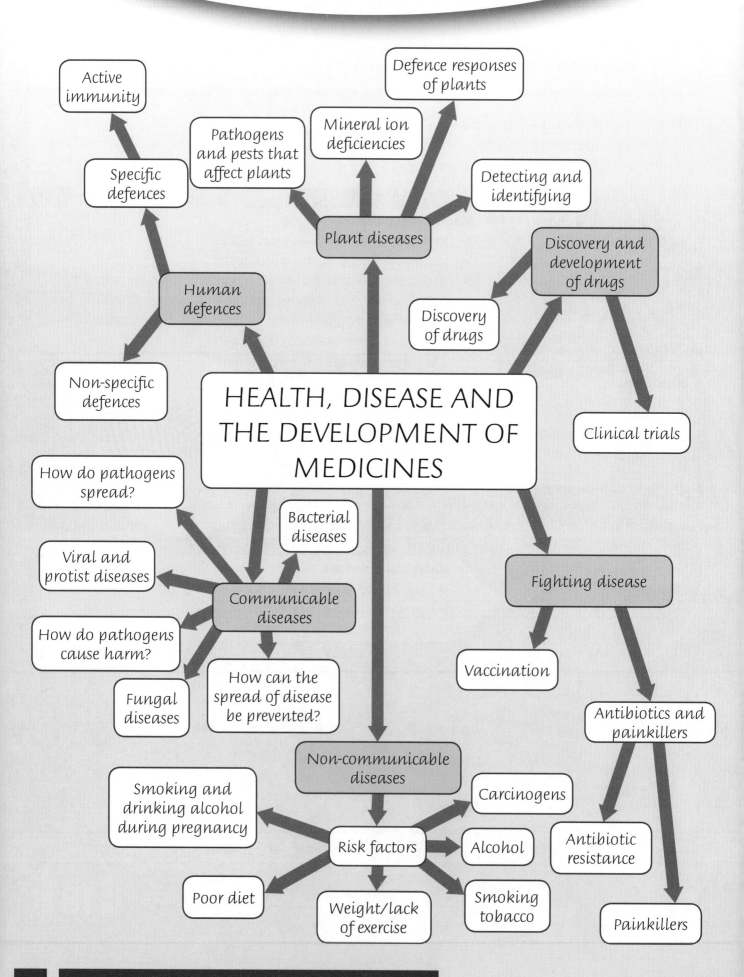

Active immunity

Specific defences

Pathogens and pests that affect plants

Mineral ion deficiencies

Defence responses of plants

Detecting and identifying

Discovery and development of drugs

Plant diseases

Human defences

Discovery of drugs

Non-specific defences

Clinical trials

HEALTH, DISEASE AND THE DEVELOPMENT OF MEDICINES

How do pathogens spread?

Bacterial diseases

Viral and protist diseases

Communicable diseases

Fighting disease

How do pathogens cause harm?

Fungal diseases

How can the spread of disease be prevented?

Vaccination

Antibiotics and painkillers

Non-communicable diseases

Smoking and drinking alcohol during pregnancy

Carcinogens

Risk factors

Alcohol

Antibiotic resistance

Poor diet

Weight/lack of exercise

Smoking tobacco

Painkillers

Practice questions

1. Draw lines to link the name of the microorganism to the disease it causes. **(3 marks)**

Bacterium		HIV
Fungus		Malaria
Virus		Cholera
Protist		Athlete's foot

2. Rani has caught flu and has been confined to bed for several days. Her mother is a health worker and was immunised against flu the previous month.

    a) Describe how the different types of blood component deal with the viruses in Rani's body.

        i)   phagocytes   **(1 mark)**

        ii) antibodies   **(1 mark)**

    b) Describe how the cells in Rani's mother's body responded to the vaccination she was given. In your answer, state what was in the vaccine and use the words **antigen**, **antibody** and **memory cells**.   **(4 marks)**

    c) After four days Rani is still unwell and she goes to the doctor. The doctor advises plenty of rest, regular intake of fluids and painkillers when necessary. Explain why the doctor doesn't prescribe antibiotics.   **(2 marks)**

    d) If Rani's symptoms continued, which other type of drug might she be prescribed?   **(1 mark)**

3. Two drugs called 'Redu' and 'DDD' have been developed to help obese people lose weight. Clinical trials are carried out on the two drugs. The results are shown in the table.

Drug	Number of volunteers in trial	Average weight loss in 6 weeks (kg)
Redu	3250	3.2
DDD	700	5.8
Placebo	2800	2.6

    a) The scientific team concluded that DDD was a more effective weight loss drug. Do you agree? Use the data in the table to give a reason for your answer.   **(2 marks)**

    b) The trial carried out was 'double blind'. Explain what this term means and why it is used. **(2 marks)**

Homeostasis and negative feedback

Keywords

Endocrine system ➤ System of ductless organs that release hormones

Stimuli ➤ Changes in the internal or external environment that affect receptors

Homeostasis

The body has automatic control systems to maintain a constant internal environment (**homeostasis**). These systems make sure that cells function efficiently.

Homeostasis balances inputs and outputs to ensure that optimal levels of temperature, pH, water, oxygen and carbon dioxide are maintained. For example, even in the cold, homeostasis ensures that body temperature is regulated at about 37°C.

Control systems in the body may involve the nervous system, the **endocrine system**, or both. There are three components of control.

➤ **Effectors** cause responses that restore optimum levels, e.g. muscles and glands.

➤ **Coordination centres** receive and process information from the receptors, e.g. brain, spinal cord and pancreas.

➤ **Receptors** detect **stimuli** from the environment, e.g. taste buds, nasal receptors, the inner ear, touch receptors and receptors on retina cells.

(WS) When taking measurements, the quality of the measuring instrument and a scientist's skill is very important to achieve **accuracy**, **precision** and **minimal error**.

Adrenaline levels in blood plasma are measured by a chromatography method called HPLC. This is often coupled to a detector that gives a digital readout.

This digital readout displays the concentration of adrenaline as 6.32. This means that the instrument is precise up to $\frac{1}{100}$ of a unit.

A less precise instrument might only measure down to $\frac{1}{10}$ of a unit, e.g. 6.3 (one decimal place).

A bar graph of some data generated from HPLC is shown below. The graph shows the **average concentration** of three different samples of blood. The average is taken from many individual measurements. The vertical error bars indicate the range of measurements (the difference between highest and lowest) obtained for each sample.

Sample C shows **the greatest precision** as the individual readings do not vary as much as the others. There is less error so we can be more confident that the average is closer to the **true value** and therefore more **accurate**.

Negative feedback

Negative feedback occurs frequently in homeostasis. It involves the automatic reversal of a change in the body's condition.

In the body, examples of negative feedback include osmoregulation/water balance, balancing blood sugar levels, maintaining a constant body temperature and controlling metabolic rate.

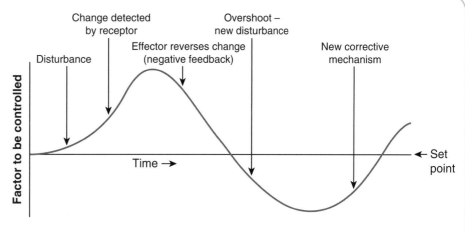

Metabolism needs to be controlled so that chemical reactions in the body take place at an optimal rate. Negative feedback controls metabolic rate by using the hormones **thyroxine** and **adrenaline**.

Thyroxine

Hypothalamus releases less TRH → Pituitary releases less TSH → Thyroid releases less thyroxine → Drop in metabolic rate

Controlling metabolic rate involves the interaction of the hormones **thyroxine**, thyroid-releasing hormone (**TRH**) and thyroid-stimulating hormone (**TSH**). Thyroxine stimulates the basal metabolic rate and plays an important role in growth and development.

Rise in metabolic rate ← Thyroid releases more thyroxine ← Pituitary releases more TSH ← Hypothalamus releases more TRH

Adrenaline

Adrenaline is sometimes called the 'flight or fight' hormone. During times of stress the adrenal glands produce adrenaline. It has a direct effect on muscles, the liver, intestines and many other organs to prepare the body for sudden bursts of energy. Specifically, adrenaline increases the heart rate so that the brain and muscles receive oxygen and glucose more rapidly.

Hypothalamus → CRH (Corticotropin-releasing hormone) → Pituitary → ACTH (Adenocorticotropic hormone) → Adrenal glands → Adrenaline

Negative feedback

HT **1.** Give two examples of negative feedback in the human body.
HT **2.** What is the target organ for the hormone CRH?

The nervous system

Structure and function

The nervous system allows organisms to react to their surroundings and coordinate their behaviour.

The two main parts of the nervous system are:
➤ the central nervous system (**CNS**), which is made up of the **spinal cord** and **brain**
➤ the **peripheral nervous system**.

The flow of **impulses** in the nervous system is carried out by nerve cells linking the receptor, coordinator (neurones and synapses in the CNS) and effector.

The main components of the nervous system

Brain

Spinal cord

The neurones that make up the peripheral nervous system

CNS (brain and spinal cord)

Sense organ	Sensory neurone	Synapse	Relay neurone	Synapse	Motor neurone	Muscle
In the sense organ, receptors detect a change – either inside or outside the body. The change is a stimulus.	Conducts the impulse from the sense organ towards the CNS.	The gap between the sensory and relay neurones.	Passes the impulse on to a motor neurone.	The gap between the relay neurone and the motor neurone.	Passes the impulse on to the muscle (or gland).	The muscle responds by contracting, which results in a movement. Muscles and glands are examples of effectors.

Nerve cells or **neurones** are specially adapted to carry nerve impulses, which are electrical in nature. The impulse is carried in the long, thin part of the cell called the **axon**.

Motor neurone

Fatty sheath

Axon

There are three types of neurone.

Sensory neurones carry impulses from receptors to the CNS.

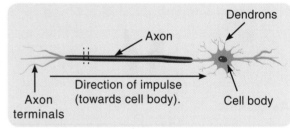

Dendrons

Axon

Axon terminals

Direction of impulse (towards cell body).

Cell body

Relay neurones make connections between neurones inside the CNS.

Dendron

Axon terminals

Impulse travels first towards, and then away from, cell body.

Motor neurones carry impulses from the CNS to muscles and glands.

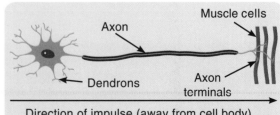

Axon

Muscle cells

Dendrons

Axon terminals

Direction of impulse (away from cell body).

🎧 **20**

Synapses

Synapses are junctions between neurones. They play an important part in regulating the way impulses are transmitted. Synapses can be found between different neurones, neurones and muscles, and between dendrites (the root-like outgrowths from the cell body).

When an impulse reaches a synapse, a **neurotransmitter** is released by the neurone ('A' in the diagram) into the gap that lies between the neurones. It travels by diffusion and binds to **receptor molecules** on the next neurone. This triggers a new electrical impulse to be released.

Neurotransmitter released here
A synapse
Impulse
Neurone A
Receptor area
Electrical impulse generated in neurone B
Cell body of neurone B

Keywords

Spinal cord ➤ Nervous tissue running down the centre of the vertebral column; millions of nerves branch out from it

Impulses ➤ Electrical signals sent down neurones that trigger responses in the nervous system

Receptor molecule ➤ Protein on the outer membrane of a cell that binds to a specific molecule, such as transmitter substance

Reflex arcs

Reflex actions:
➤ are involuntary/automatic
➤ are very rapid
➤ protect the body from harm
➤ bypass conscious thought.

The pathway taken by impulses around the body is called a **reflex arc**. Examples include:
➤ opening and closing the pupil in the eye
➤ the knee-jerk response
➤ withdrawing your hand from a hot plate.

Here is the arc pathway for a pain response.

❸ Relay neurone
Spinal cord
❺ Effector (muscle)
❹ Motor neurone
❷ Sensory neurone
Drawing pin (stimulus)
❶ Receptor

WS You may have to investigate the effect of factors on human reaction time.

For example, you could be asked to investigate a learned reflex by measuring how far up a ruler someone can catch it. The nearer to the zero the ruler is caught, the faster the reflex.

You could investigate factors such as:
➤ experience/practice at catching
➤ sound ➤ touch ➤ sight.

Can you design experiments to test these variables? Which factors will need to be kept the same?

1. Name the long, thin extensions of nerve cells.
2. How do reflex arcs aid survival of an organism?
3. Design and draw a flow diagram to represent the pathway followed by impulses in the knee-jerk reflex. (The flow diagram at the beginning of this module should help you.)

Nervous control

🎧 21

Keywords

Neuroscience ➤ Study of the nervous system

Dermis ➤ The layer of tissue in the skin that lies beneath the epidermis. It contains many receptors and structures involved in temperature control

Epidermis ➤ Outer layer of tissue in the skin

The brain

The brain is part of the central nervous system (**CNS**) and is studied by **neuroscientists**. The brain controls many activities in the body but is also responsible for memory, learning and behaviour.

The brain is made up of billions of neurones, each interlinked via synapses. There are four main parts of the brain.

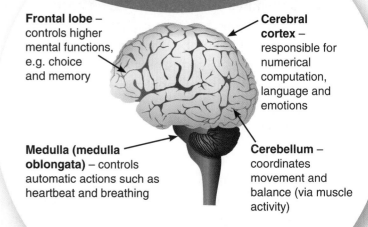

Frontal lobe – controls higher mental functions, e.g. choice and memory

Cerebral cortex – responsible for numerical computation, language and emotions

Medulla (medulla oblongata) – controls automatic actions such as heartbeat and breathing

Cerebellum – coordinates movement and balance (via muscle activity)

HT Studying the brain

Neuroscientists have mapped the regions of the brain to different functions. This is particularly useful for studying people suffering from brain damage and brain disorders, such as Alzheimer's disease. Studying healthy volunteers, using MRI technology and electrical stimulation of different parts of the brain, can reveal information about how this complex organ works.

Problems with studying and treating brain function include:
➤ obtaining subjects to study
➤ ethical issues relating to using human subjects
➤ difficulty when interpreting case studies
➤ difficulty in accessing areas of the brain where damage has occurred.

When treating nerve damage, the prospects can be limited because nervous and surrounding tissues are difficult to repair.

Scanning the brain

CT or **CAT** scans (computerised axial tomography) are X-ray tests producing cross-sectional images of the brain using computer programs. Many images can be taken at different angles to create 3D pictures.

PET stands for positron emission tomography. A PET scan can show what body tissues look like and how they are working. PET scanners work by detecting radiation given off by radiotracers, which the patient takes orally. The tracers accumulate in particular areas of the body. PET is often combined with CT and MRI technology to give 3D views of the brain.

Controlling body temperature

The thermoregulatory centre in the brain monitors and controls body temperature.

As you found out in Module 6, enzymes work at around **37°C** (core temperature for humans). It is essential that this temperature does not fluctuate too much. Body heat is released by chemical reactions in the body (metabolism) and distributed via the bloodstream.

The skin plays a major role in temperature regulation. The structures responsible are found in the **dermis** and **epidermis** of the skin.

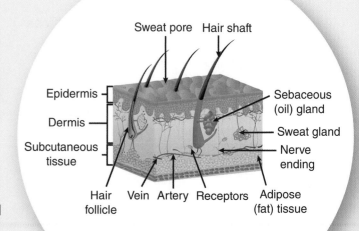

Sweat pore   Hair shaft

Epidermis

Dermis

Subcutaneous tissue

Hair follicle   Vein   Artery   Receptors   Adipose (fat) tissue

Sebaceous (oil) gland

Sweat gland

Nerve ending

When core temperature falls

➤ There is reduced blood flow near the skin to limit heat loss to the environment. This is called **vasoconstriction**.

➤ Tiny involuntary contractions of muscles (shivering) generate heat.

➤ Sweating reduces.

➤ Body hairs rise due to the contraction of special muscles. Humans have less body hair than most mammals so there is minimal benefit.

When core temperature rises

➤ Blood flows closer to the skin surface because blood vessels widen. This is called **vasodilation**.

➤ Sweating increases. The sweat evaporates on the skin's surface, which absorbs heat from the skin in an **endothermic** change.

➤ Body hairs lower.

Reduced blood flow through superficial capillaries — Sweating stopped — Sweat gland — Shunt vessel open

Greater blood flow through superficial capillaries — Heat loss by radiation — Sweat — Sweat gland — Shunt vessel closed

Negative feedback system

There is a negative feedback system for regulating body temperature.

Increase → Detected by thermoreceptors in skin and hypothalamus → Cooling mechanisms: sweating and vasodilation → Decrease

Normal body temperature

Normal body temperature

Increase ← Heating mechanisms: shivering and vasoconstriction ← Detected by thermoreceptors in skin and hypothalamus ← Decrease

In this control system we have:

➤ receptors – thermoreceptors in the skin

➤ a controller – hypothalamus in the brain

➤ effectors – a variety of organs and tissues.

If a control system breaks down it can be life-threatening.

➤ **Hypothermia** is when the body temperature falls well below 37°C. Symptoms include shivering, blue skin colour, disorientation and unconsciousness.

➤ **Heat stroke/dehydration** is when the body temperature rises well above 37°C. Symptoms include an altered mental state, nausea, flushed skin, and rapid breathing and pulse.

➤ Create two identical plasticine models showing the main parts of the skin involved in temperature control. Use different colours for each of the structures.

➤ Modify one of your models to show what happens if body temperature is rising, and the other one to show what happens when body temperature falls below normal. In particular, try to show what happens to the blood vessels during vasodilation and vasoconstriction.

1. Which part of the brain is responsible for learning, thinking and memory?

HT 2. State the main differences between a CT scan and a PET scan.

3. Describe how structures in the skin respond when core body temperature rises.

The eye

Structure

The eye is a major sense organ in the human body. The receptors are on the **retina** – they consist of light-sensitive cells that detect the intensity and colour of light that enters the eye.

Light-sensitive cells are of two types – rods and cones. Rods are sensitive to low light intensities and enable vision in black and white. Cones are less sensitive and operate at higher light intensities. They enable us to see in colour. The three types of cone are those sensitive to:

➤ red light
➤ green light
➤ blue light.

Light entering the eye is perceived as a certain colour because these three types of cone are stimulated to different degrees, resulting in many millions of different shades and hues.

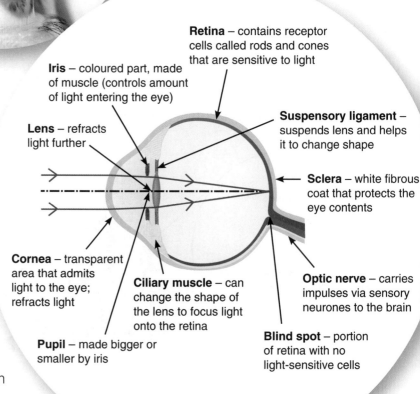

Retina – contains receptor cells called rods and cones that are sensitive to light

Iris – coloured part, made of muscle (controls amount of light entering the eye)

Lens – refracts light further

Suspensory ligament – suspends lens and helps it to change shape

Sclera – white fibrous coat that protects the eye contents

Cornea – transparent area that admits light to the eye; refracts light

Ciliary muscle – can change the shape of the lens to focus light onto the retina

Optic nerve – carries impulses via sensory neurones to the brain

Pupil – made bigger or smaller by iris

Blind spot – portion of retina with no light-sensitive cells

Accommodation

The function of the eye is to receive light rays and focus them to form a sharp image on the retina. The optical information is sent to the brain, which interprets it to give a sense of a 3D image, movement, colour and brightness. This interpretation by the occipital lobe in the brain is called **perception**.

The focusing process is called **accommodation**. It involves changing the shape of the lens in order to refract light.

To focus on a **near object**: ➤ light rays **diverge** significantly ➤ the ciliary muscles **contract** ➤ the suspensory ligaments loosen/go **slack** ➤ the lens becomes **short** and **fat** (**more** convex) ➤ the direction of light rays changes **greatly** to converge on the retina.	
To focus on a distant object: ➤ light rays are almost parallel ➤ the ciliary muscles **relax** ➤ the suspensory ligaments become **taut** ➤ the lens becomes **long** and **thin** (**less convex**) ➤ the direction of light rays changes **slightly** to converge on the retina.	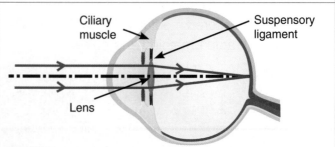

This is the front view of what happens during accommodation.

Near object

Suspensory ligaments slack

Ciliary muscles contracted

Lens more spherical

Distant object

Suspensory ligaments pulled taut

Ciliary muscles relaxed

Lens flat and thin

Keywords

Diverge ➤ Spread outwards from a point

Convex ➤ Lens that curves inwards on one or both sides

Converge ➤ Come together at a point

Concave ➤ Lens that curves outwards on one or both sides

Defects

Common eye defects are:

➤ hyperopia (long sightedness)
➤ myopia (short sightedness)
➤ red–green colour blindness
➤ cataracts.

Cataract

Hyperopia and **myopia** can be corrected using spectacles, contact lenses or laser surgery (to change the shape of the cornea).

Hyperopia is:

➤ caused by an eyeball that is too short, or a lens that stays too long and thin
➤ corrected by a **convex** lens.

Myopia is:

➤ caused by an eyeball that is too long, or weak suspensory ligaments that cannot pull the lens into a thin shape
➤ corrected by a **concave** lens.

Red–green colour blindness is more common in boys as it is determined by a defective gene on the X chromosome. The result is one or more cone types being faulty, causing an inability to distinguish between different shades of red or green.

A **cataract** develops when the lens clouds over. This is caused by some of the protein in the lens clumping together. Using spectacles with strong bifocals is a temporary treatment. The only permanent solution is removal during surgery.

An alternative to spectacles is **contact lenses**. These are miniature lenses (either hard or soft) that can be placed over the front of the eye. They need to be kept clean if they are a permanent type, or disposed of if temporary. Some operations can replace the natural lens with a new one.

(WS) You will be expected to give examples of how scientific ideas can lead to technical applications. The development of optical instruments for helping vision is a good example.

Sir Isaac Newton developed laws of optics in the seventeenth century. This built on theories put forward by scientists previously. An understanding of how light is refracted and reflected, and of ray diagrams, has led to inventions such as telescopes, microscopes and spectacles.

22

1. Which part of the eye controls the amount of light entering it?
2. Describe the shape of the lens when the eye is focusing on an object a short distance away.
3. What causes hyperopia?

The endocrine system

Keywords

Ductless gland ➤ A gland that does not secrete its chemicals through a tube. The pancreas is an exception to this rule as it contains a duct for delivering enzymes, but its hormones are released directly into the bloodstream

Glucagon ➤ Hormone released by the pancreas that stimulates the conversion of glycogen to glucose

Glycogen ➤ Storage carbohydrate found in animals

Structure and function

The endocrine system is made up of glands that are **ductless** and secrete **hormones** directly into the bloodstream. The blood carries these chemical messengers to **target organs** around the body, where they cause an effect.

Hormones:
➤ are large, protein molecules
➤ interact with the nervous system to exert control over essential biological processes
➤ act over a longer time period than nervous responses but their effects are slower to establish.

Endocrine gland	Hormone(s) produced
Pituitary gland	TSH, ADH, FSH, LH, etc.
Pancreas	Insulin, **glucagon**
Thyroid	Thyroxine
Adrenal gland	Adrenaline
Ovaries (female)	Oestrogen, progesterone
Testes (male)	Testosterone

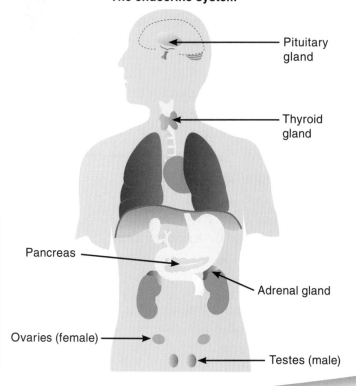

The endocrine system

- Pituitary gland
- Thyroid gland
- Pancreas
- Adrenal gland
- Ovaries (female)
- Testes (male)

Pituitary gland

The pituitary gland

The pituitary is often referred to as the **master gland** because it secretes many hormones that control other processes in the body. Pituitary hormones often trigger other hormones to be released.

➤ Create a series of flashcards about controlling blood glucose levels. On each one, write a hormone, organ or effect relating to the control system. Shuffle the cards and put them face down.
➤ With a revision buddy, or on your own, pick up each card and explain how the particular component is involved in the control process.

Controlling blood glucose concentration

The control system for balancing blood glucose levels involves the **pancreas**.

The pancreas monitors the blood glucose concentration and releases hormones to restore the balance. When the concentration is too high, the pancreas produces insulin that causes glucose to be absorbed from the blood by all body cells, but particularly those in the liver and muscles. These organs convert glucose to **glycogen** for storage until required.

Blood glucose concentration is too high

The pancreas releases insulin

Glucose is converted to insoluble glycogen stored in the liver and muscles

Blood glucose concentration returns to normal

Glucose is removed from the blood

HT If blood glucose concentration is too low, the pancreas secretes glucagon. This stimulates the conversion of glycogen to glucose via enzymic systems. It is then released into the blood.

Glucose in blood

Insulin

Glucagon

Liver

Glycogen

Glycogen

Muscles

Diabetes

There are two types of diabetes.

Type I diabetes:
- ➤ is caused by the pancreas' inability to produce insulin
- ➤ results in dangerously high levels of blood glucose
- ➤ is controlled by delivery of insulin into the bloodstream via injection or a 'patch' worn on the skin
- ➤ is more likely to occur in people under 40
- ➤ is the most common type of diabetes in childhood
- ➤ is thought to be triggered by an auto-immune response where cells in the pancreas are destroyed.

Type II diabetes:
- ➤ is caused by fatty deposits preventing body cells from absorbing insulin; the pancreas tries to compensate by producing more and more insulin until it is unable to produce any more
- ➤ results in dangerously high levels of blood glucose
- ➤ is controlled by a low carbohydrate diet and exercise initially; it may require insulin in the later stages
- ➤ is more common in people over 40
- ➤ is a risk factor if you are obese.

1. Why is the pituitary called the master gland?
2. Where are the sex hormones of the body produced?
3. What effects does type II diabetes have on the body?

Excretion

Excretion is the process of getting rid of waste products made by chemical reactions in the body. Don't confuse it with **egestion**, which is the loss of solid waste (mainly undigested food).

The following are excreted products.

➤ **Urea** is made from the breakdown of excess amino acids in the liver. It is removed by the kidneys along with excess water and ions and transferred to the bladder as **urine** before being released.

➤ **Sweat** containing water, urea and salt is excreted by sweat glands onto the surface of the skin. Sweating aids the body's cooling process.

➤ **Carbon dioxide** and **water** are produced by respiration and leave the body from the lungs during exhalation.

The lungs and skin don't control the loss of substances. They are simply the organs by which these substances are removed.

Water & nitrogen balance

The kidneys

Vena cava Aorta

Kidney (filtration and reabsorption)

Renal artery ⎫ Blood supply
Renal vein ⎬ to and from
            ⎭ the kidneys

Bladder (stores urine)

Ureter (carries urine from kidney to bladder)

Urethra (carries urine from bladder to outside)

The kidneys filter the blood, allowing urea to pass to the bladder. The filtering is carried out within the kidney by thousands of tiny **kidney tubules**.

Kidney tubules

Capillary   Tubule

Water
Ions
Urea
Sugar

Water ❸
Ions
Sugar
    ❹

Most of the water, ions and all sugar | Excess water, ions and all urea

❶ **Filtration**
Lots of water plus all the small molecules are squeezed out of the blood, under pressure, into the tubules.

❷ **Selective reabsorption**
Useful substances, including glucose, ions and water, are reabsorbed into the blood from the tubules.

❸ **Osmoregulation**
Amount of water in the blood and urine is adjusted here.

❹ **Excretion of waste**
Excess water, ions and all the urea now pass to the bladder in the form of urine and are eventually released from the body.

Other useful substances (glucose, amino acids, fatty acids, glycerol and some water) are **selectively re-absorbed** early in the process.

The kidneys also control the balance of water in the blood. Damage occurs to red blood cells if water content is not balanced.

Ideal shape	Swollen	Shrivelled
When red blood cells (erythrocytes) are in solutions with equal concentration to their cytoplasm, they have an ideal, biconcave shape. This is because there is no net movement of water in or out.	When immersed in a solution of lower concentration (higher water concentration), the cells absorb water by osmosis. The weak cell membrane cannot resist the added water pressure and may burst.	In a more concentrated solution (lower water concentration), cells lose water by osmosis. They shrivel up and become **crenated** (have scalloped edges).

Kidney tubules (nephrons)

In terms of nephron structure, filtration, selective reabsorption and excretion of waste occur in the following regions.

Structure of the nephron

Blood under pressure containing waste substances

Bowman's capsule Convoluted tubules

Glomerulus

Capillary networks

Loop of Henlé

Collecting ducts (lead to the ureter)

❶ Filtration, where all small molecules and lots of water are squeezed out of the blood and into the tubules.

❷ Selective reabsorption of useful substances (water, ions, glucose) back into the blood from the convoluted tubules. This may take energy in the case of glucose and ions.

❸ Excretion of waste in the form of excess water, excess ions and all urea. These drain into the collecting tubules and pass to the bladder as urine.

Kidney failure

Kidneys may fail due to accidents or disease. A patient can survive with one kidney. If both kidneys are affected, two treatments are available.

Kidney transplant – involves a healthy person donating one kidney to replace two failed kidneys in another person.

Dialysis – offered to patients while they wait for the possibility of a kidney transplant. A dialysis machine removes urea and maintains levels of sodium and glucose in the blood.

This is what happens during dialysis.

1. Blood is taken from a person's vein and run into the dialysis machine, where it comes into close contact with a **partially permeable membrane**.
2. This separates the blood from the dialysis fluid.
3. The urea and other waste diffuse from the blood into the dialysis fluid. The useful substances remain and are transferred back to the body.

Blood from patient — Blood returned to patient

Urea — Excess substances — Partially permeable membrane

Dialysis fluid — Waste fluid

24

Keywords

Urea ➤ Nitrogenous waste product

Selective re-absorption ➤ Occurs in the kidney tubules and allows useful substances to pass from the kidneys back into the blood

Partially permeable membrane ➤ Artificial or organic layer that only allows small molecules through

HT **Deamination** ➤ Process in the liver in which nitrogen is removed from an amino acid molecule

HT **Ammonia** ➤ Nitrogenous waste product

HT How urea is formed

Proteins obtained from the diet may produce a surplus of **amino acids** that need to be excreted safely.

1. First, the amino acids are **deaminated** in the **liver** to form **ammonia**.
2. Ammonia is toxic so is immediately converted to urea, which is then filtered out in the kidney.

Controlling water content

The osmotic balance of the body's fluids needs to be tightly controlled because if cells gain or lose too much water they do not function efficiently.

The amount of water re-absorbed by the kidneys is controlled by **anti-diuretic hormone (ADH)**. This is produced in the pituitary.

1. ADH directly increases the permeability of the kidney tubules to water.
2. When the water content of the blood is low (higher blood concentration), **negative feedback** operates to restore normal levels.

The effect of ADH on blood water content

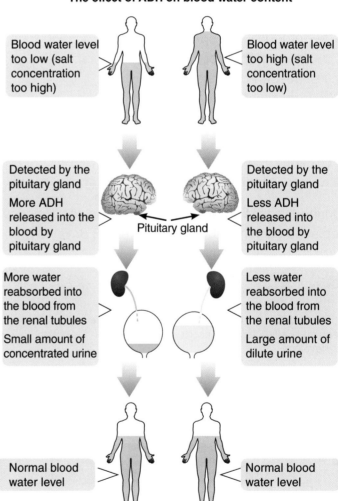

Blood water level too low (salt concentration too high)

Blood water level too high (salt concentration too low)

Detected by the pituitary gland

More ADH released into the blood by pituitary gland

Pituitary gland

Detected by the pituitary gland

Less ADH released into the blood by pituitary gland

More water reabsorbed into the blood from the renal tubules

Small amount of concentrated urine

Less water reabsorbed into the blood from the renal tubules

Large amount of dilute urine

Normal blood water level

Normal blood water level

1. List three substances that are selectively re-absorbed back into the bloodstream from the kidney.
HT 2. What effect does producing **more** ADH have on the concentration of urine?
3. Describe what happens to a urea molecule as it passes through a dialysis machine.

Hormones in human reproduction

Hormones play a vital role in regulating human reproduction, especially in the female **menstrual** cycle.

Puberty

During **puberty** (approximately 10–16 in girls and 12–17 in boys), the sex organs begin to produce **sex hormones**. This causes the development of **secondary sexual characteristics**.

In **males**, the primary sex hormone is **testosterone**.

During puberty, testosterone is produced from the testes and causes:
➤ production of sperm in testes
➤ development of muscles and penis
➤ deepening of the voice
➤ growth of pubic, facial and body hair.

In **females**, the primary sex hormone is **oestrogen**. Other sex hormones are **progesterone**, **FSH** and **LH**.

During puberty, oestrogen is produced in the ovaries and progesterone production starts when the menstrual cycle begins.

The secondary sexual characteristics are:
➤ ovulation and the menstrual cycle
➤ breast growth
➤ widening of hips
➤ growth of pubic and armpit hair.

The menstrual cycle

A woman is fertile between the ages of approximately 13 and 50.

During this time, an egg is released from one of her ovaries each month and the lining of her uterus is replaced each month (approximately 28 days) to prepare for pregnancy.

The menstrual cycle

Ovary

Follicle with egg gradually develops

Ovulation (egg released)

Empty follicle gradually disappears

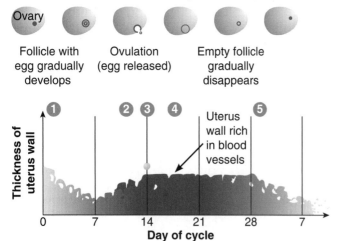

Uterus wall rich in blood vessels

1 Uterus lining breaks down (i.e. a period).
2 Repair of the uterus wall. Oestrogen causes the uterus lining to gradually thicken.
3 Egg released by the ovary.
4 Progesterone and oestrogen make the lining stay thick, waiting for a fertilised egg.
5 No fertilised egg so cycle restarts.

Oestrogen

Progesterone

As well as oestrogen and progesterone, the two other hormones involved in the cycle are:

➤ **FSH** or **follicle stimulating hormone**, which causes maturation of an egg in the ovary
➤ **LH** or **luteinising hormone**, which stimulates release of an egg.

Negative feedback in the menstrual cycle

The four female hormones interact in a complex manner to regulate the cycle.

➤ **FSH** is produced in the pituitary and acts on the ovaries, causing an egg to mature. It **stimulates** the ovaries to produce oestrogen.
➤ **Oestrogen** is secreted in the ovaries and **inhibits** further production of FSH. It also **stimulates** the release of LH and promotes repair of the uterus wall after menstruation.
➤ **LH** is produced in the pituitary. It also **stimulates** release of an egg.
➤ **Progesterone** is secreted by the empty **follicle** in the ovary (left by the egg). It **maintains** the lining of the uterus after ovulation has occurred. It also **inhibits** FSH and LH.

HT

Female reproductive system

Low progesterone levels allow FSH from the pituitary gland to stimulate the maturation of an egg (in a follicle). This in turn stimulates oestrogen production.

High levels of oestrogen stimulate a surge in LH from the pituitary gland. This triggers ovulation in the middle of the cycle.

Brain

Pituitary gland

Ovary — Uterus — Ovary

Keywords

Menstruation ➤ Loss of blood and muscle tissue from the uterus wall during the monthly cycle

Follicle stimulating hormone ➤ A hormone produced by the pituitary gland that controls oestrogen production by the ovaries

HT **Inhibition** ➤ Negative effect in negative feedback, where the increase in one factor brings a **decrease** in another

25

To familiarise yourself with what the various hormones do in the menstrual cycle, you may find it helpful to do the following.

➤ On a computer, create a series of text boxes listing the organs, hormones and effects relating to the menstrual cycle. You could also include diagrams of the organs.
➤ Re-arrange the text boxes/diagrams so they are out of order.
➤ Test yourself or ask a revision buddy to put them back in the correct position/order. Alternatively, you could draw or write the organs, hormones and effects on paper and re-arrange them manually.

1. Name the four hormones involved in the menstrual cycle. What are their functions?
2. At approximately what stage in the menstrual cycle does the uterus lining repair itself?
3. Name one effect of testosterone in puberty.

Contraception and infertility

Fertility and the possibility of pregnancy can be controlled using non-hormonal and hormonal methods of **contraception**.

Keywords

Contraception ➤ Literally means 'against conception'; any method that reduces the likelihood of a sperm meeting an egg

Intrauterine ➤ Inside the uterus

Implantation ➤ Process in which an embryo embeds itself in the uterine wall

Oral contraceptive ➤ Hormonal contraceptive taken in tablet form

Non-hormonal contraception

Contraceptive method	Method of action	Advantages	Disadvantages
➤ Barrier method – condom (male + female)	Prevents the sperm from reaching the egg	82% effective ➤ Most effective against STIs	➤ Can only be used once ➤ May interrupt sexual activity ➤ Can break ➤ Women may be allergic to latex
➤ Barrier method – diaphragm	Prevents the sperm from reaching the egg	88% effective ➤ Can be put in place right before intercourse or 2–3 hours before ➤ Don't need to take out between acts of sexual intercourse	➤ Increases urinary tract infections ➤ Doesn't protect against STIs
➤ **Intrauterine** device	Prevents **implantation** – some release hormones	99% effective ➤ Very effective against pregnancy ➤ Doesn't need daily attention ➤ Comfortable ➤ Can be removed at any time	➤ Doesn't protect against STIs ➤ Needs to be inserted by a medical practitioner ➤ Higher risk of infection when first inserted ➤ Can have side effects such as menstrual cramping ➤ Can fall out and puncture the uterus (rare)
➤ Spermicidal agent	Kills or disables sperm	72% effective ➤ Cheap	➤ Doesn't protect against STIs ➤ Needs to be reapplied after one hour ➤ Increases urinary tract infections ➤ Some people are allergic to spermicidal agents
➤ Abstinence ➤ Calendar method	Refraining from sexual intercourse when an egg is likely to be in the oviduct	76% effective ➤ Natural ➤ Approved by many religions ➤ Woman gets to know her body and menstrual cycles	➤ Doesn't protect against STIs ➤ Calculating the ovulation period each month requires careful monitoring and instruction ➤ Can't have sexual intercourse for at least a week each month
➤ Surgical method	Vasectomy and female sterilisation	99% effective ➤ Very effective against pregnancy ➤ One-time decision providing permanent protection	➤ No protection against STIs ➤ Need to have minor surgery ➤ Permanent

Hormonal contraception

Contraceptive method	Method of action	Advantages	Disadvantages
➤ Oral contraceptive	Contains hormones that inhibit FSH production, so eggs fail to mature	91% effectiveness ➤ Very effective against pregnancy if used correctly ➤ Makes menstrual periods lighter and more regular ➤ Lowers risk of ovarian and uterine cancer, and other conditions ➤ Doesn't interrupt sexual activity	➤ Doesn't protect against STIs ➤ Need to remember to take it every day at the same time ➤ Can't be used by women with certain medical problems or by women taking certain medications ➤ Can occasionally cause side effects
➤ Hormone injection ➤ Skin patch ➤ Implant	Provides slow release of progesterone; this inhibits maturation and release of eggs	91–99% effectiveness depending on method used ➤ Lasts over many months or years ➤ Light or no menstrual periods ➤ Doesn't interrupt sexual activity	➤ Doesn't protect against STIs ➤ May require minor surgery (for implant) ➤ Can cause side effects

The percentage figures in the contraception tables are based on users in a whole population, regardless of whether they use the method correctly. If consistently used correctly, the percentage effectiveness of each method is usually higher. Some methods, such as the calendar method, are more prone to error than others.

HT Infertility treatment

Infertility treatment is used by couples who have problems conceiving.

Reasons for infertility

No eggs being released from the ovaries.
Endometriosis, which occurs when the tissue that lines the inside of the uterus enters other organs of the body, such as the abdomen and fallopian tubes; this reduces the maturation rate and release of eggs.
Male infertility/low sperm count.
Uterine fibroids.
Complete or partial blocking and/or scarring of the fallopian tubes.
Reduced number and quality of eggs.

Methods of treatment

Treating infertility is known as ART (assisted reproductive technology). There are a number of methods of treatment.

➤ **Fertility drugs** containing FSH and LH are given to women who do not produce enough FSH themselves. They may then become pregnant naturally.

➤ **Clomifene therapy** prevents the production of oestrogen and so inhibits negative feedback.

➤ **In vitro fertilisation (IVF)** is a method in which the potential mother is given FSH and

LH to stimulate the production of several eggs. Sperm is collected from the father. The sperm and eggs are then introduced together outside the body in a petri dish. One or two growing embryos can then be transplanted into the woman's uterus.

IVF under a microscope

Injected with father's sperm

Holds the egg in place

Unfertilised human egg cell

Disadvantages of IVF

It is very expensive.
It can be mentally and physically stressful.
Success rates are only approximately 40% (at the time of writing).
There is an increased risk of multiple births.

1. Which contraceptives might not be suitable for a woman suffering from high blood pressure?
2. Why are condoms effective against the spread of HIV?
HT 3. How has the development of microscopy helped couples with infertility problems?

Plant hormones

Tropisms and general control

Plants, as well as animals, respond to changes in their environment.

Plant hormones are chemicals that control the growth of shoots and roots, flowering and the ripening of fruits.

Two major groups of hormones are:
➤ auxins
➤ gibberellins.

These hormones move through the plant in solution and affect its growth by responding to:
➤ gravity (**gravitropism/geotropism**)
➤ light (**phototropism**).

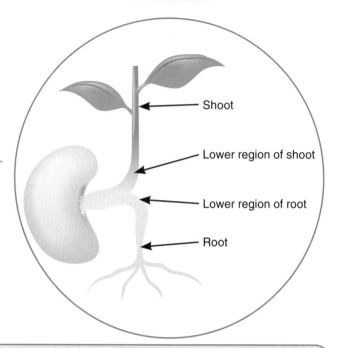

- Shoot
- Lower region of shoot
- Lower region of root
- Root

Geotropism

Root

Auxin moves to this side – growth is inhibited so root grows downwards

Response to gravity
➤ **Shoots** grow **against** gravity (**negative gravitropism**).
➤ **Roots** grow **in the direction of gravity** (**positive gravitropism**).

In the roots, auxins inhibit growth in the lower region, which makes the roots grow downwards. The roots anchor the plant in the soil and seek out water and minerals for absorption.

Response to light
➤ **Roots** grow **away** from the light (**negative tropism**).
➤ **Shoots** grow **towards** the light (**positive tropism**).

In the shoot, auxin is made in the tip. When light reaches the tip from all directions, the hormone is equally distributed. When light is **uni-directional** (in this case from the right), the auxin moves to the shaded side, causing the cells here to **elongate**. This makes the shoot bend towards the light.

Phototropism

Auxin moves to this side – cells elongate and the shoot bends towards the light

Unidirectional light

Plant shoot

Commercial uses of hormones

Auxins

- ➤ **Rooting powder** consists of an auxin that encourages the growth of roots in stem cuttings, so that many new plants can be grown from a parent.
- ➤ **Tissue culture** technique also requires auxins to promote growth.
- ➤ **Selective weed killers**, used in agriculture, contain auxins that disrupt the growth patterns of their target plants (which are often broad-leaved rather than narrow-leaved). Therefore the crop plant is not harmed.

Gibberellins

Gibberellins are important in initiating **seed germination**. They can be used to:

- ➤ end seed dormancy
- ➤ promote flowering
- ➤ increase fruit size
- ➤ produce seedless fruit (parthenocarpy).

Ethene

Ethene is a hydrocarbon that controls cell division. It can be used in the food industry to **control ripening of fruit** while it is being transported or stored.

Keywords

Gravitropism (geotropism) ➤ Growth response in plants against or with the force of gravity

Phototropism ➤ Growth response in plants, towards or away from the direction of incoming light

 One of your required practicals is likely to be investigating the effect of light on the growth of newly germinated shoots.

This is one possible investigation. What other investigations could you carry out?

Experiment to show that shoots grow towards light

① Cut a hole in the side of a box. Put three cuttings into the box. The cuttings detect light coming from the hole and will grow towards it.

② Cut a hole in the side of another box. Put three cuttings with foil-covered tips in the box. These shoots can't detect the light so they grow straight up.

---

 1. What differences would you notice between roots and shoots in the way they respond to increased auxin levels?

HT 2. Which hormones could a farmer apply to her crop to increase the yield?

HT 3. Which hormone could be used to cause plants to flower early?

Mind map

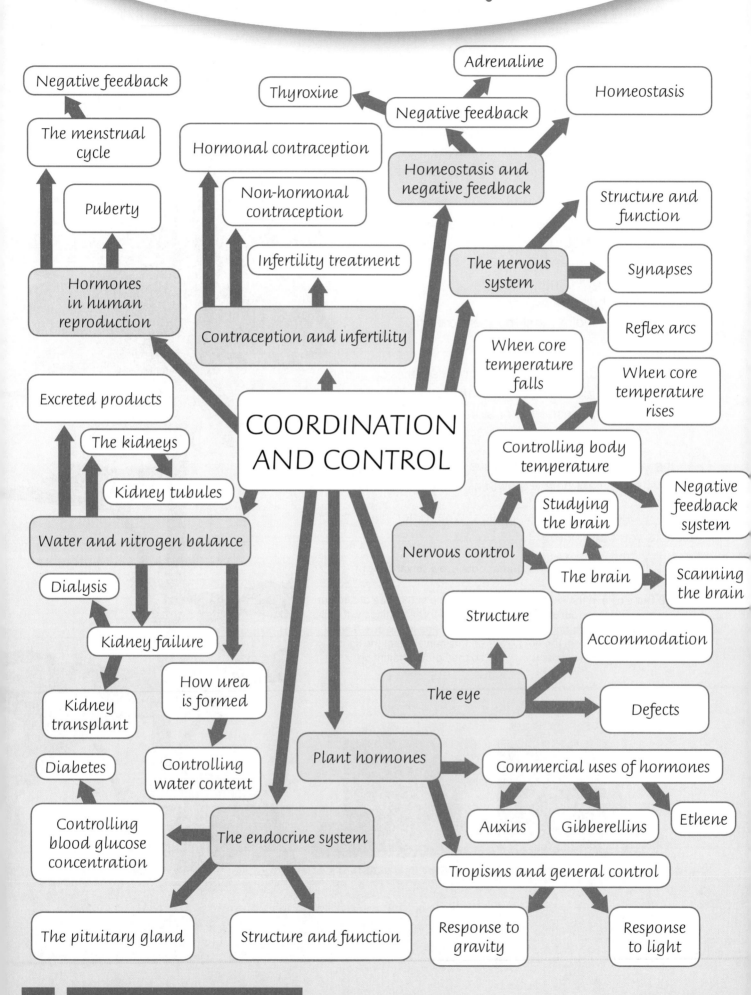

Negative feedback

The menstrual cycle

Thyroxine

Hormonal contraception

Adrenaline

Negative feedback

Homeostasis

Puberty

Non-hormonal contraception

Homeostasis and negative feedback

Structure and function

Hormones in human reproduction

Infertility treatment

The nervous system

Synapses

Contraception and infertility

Reflex arcs

Excreted products

When core temperature falls

When core temperature rises

The kidneys

COORDINATION AND CONTROL

Kidney tubules

Controlling body temperature

Negative feedback system

Water and nitrogen balance

Nervous control

Studying the brain

Dialysis

The brain

Scanning the brain

Kidney failure

Kidney transplant

How urea is formed

Structure

Accommodation

Diabetes

Controlling water content

The eye

Defects

Controlling blood glucose concentration

The endocrine system

Plant hormones

Commercial uses of hormones

Auxins

Gibberellins

Ethene

The pituitary gland

Structure and function

Tropisms and general control

Response to gravity

Response to light

Practice questions

1. The flow chart shows the events that occur during a reflex action.

| X | Receptor | Sensory neurone | Relay neurone in brain or spinal cord | Motor neurone | Effector |

Paul accidentally puts his hand on a pin. Without thinking, he immediately pulls his hand away.

    a)   Which component of a reflex arc is represented by the letter X?   **(1 mark)**

    b)   Give **two** reasons why this can be described as a reflex action.   **(2 marks)**

    c)   Use the flow chart to describe what happens in this reflex action.   **(4 marks)**

2. Look at the graph showing a person's blood sugar levels.

    a)   How can we tell from the graph that this person has diabetes?   **(2 marks)**

    b)   Explain why the person's blood sugar level rises rapidly just after points A and B.   **(1 mark)**

    c)   Describe what would happen after points A and B if the person did not have diabetes.   **(1 mark)**

    d)   Explain why the person needed to eat a chocolate at point C.   **(1 mark)**

3. Penny is exercising. Many changes are happening in her body. Sweat glands help to control her temperature.

    a)   Explain how the sweat glands help to control the temperature of her body.   **(2 marks)**

    b)   As Penny exercises, she produces carbon dioxide in her cells. What name is given to the process that converts substances into waste products?   **(1 mark)**

    c)   Penny's liver produces urea. Which substances are changed to form urea?   **(1 mark)**

    d)   Penny's kidneys process the urea. The route the urea follows is shown below. Write down the missing stages.   **(2 marks)**

| Urea produced in liver | → | | → | Urea filtered in the kidneys |
| Urea in urine passes out of body | ← | | ← | Urine passes down ureter |

Sexual and asexual reproduction

One of the basic characteristics of life is **reproduction**. This is the means by which a species continues. If sufficient offspring are not produced, the species becomes **extinct**.

Sexual reproduction

Sexual reproduction is where a male **gamete** (e.g. sperm) meets a female gamete (e.g. egg). This **fusion** of the two gametes is called **fertilisation** and may be internal or external.

Gametes are produced by **meiosis** in the sex organs (see Module 4).

Asexual reproduction

Sexual reproduction

Egg (haploid gamete)   Sperm (haploid gamete)

Fertilisation

Nucleus contains a mixture of genes from both parents

Fertilised egg (diploid zygote)

Asexual reproduction

Asexual reproduction does not require different male and female cells. Instead, genetically identical clones are produced from mitosis. These may just be individual cells, as in the case of yeast, or whole multicellular organisms, e.g. aphids.

Many organisms can reproduce using both methods, depending on the environmental conditions.

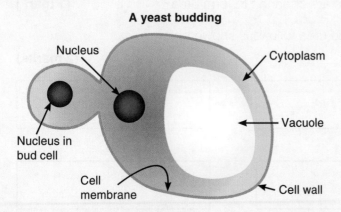

A yeast budding

Nucleus

Cytoplasm

Nucleus in bud cell

Vacuole

Cell membrane

Cell wall

Comparing sexual and asexual reproduction

Advantages of sexual reproduction

➤ Produces **variation** in offspring through the process of meiosis, where genes are 'shuffled.' Variation is increased by **random fusion of gametes**.
➤ Survival advantage gained when the environment changes because different genetic types have more chance of producing well-adapted offspring.
➤ Humans can make use of sexual reproduction through **selective breeding**. This enhances food production.

Disadvantages of sexual reproduction

➤ Relatively slow process.
➤ Variation can be a disadvantage in stable environments.
➤ More resources required than for asexual reproduction, e.g. energy, time.
➤ Results of selective breeding are unpredictable and might lead to genetic abnormalities from 'in-breeding'.

Advantages of asexual reproduction

➤ Only one parent required.
➤ Fewer resources (energy and time) need to be devoted to finding a mate.
➤ Faster than sexual reproduction – survival advantage of producing many offspring in a short period of time.
➤ Many identical offspring of a well-adapted individual can be produced to take advantage of favourable conditions.

Disadvantages of asexual reproduction

➤ Offspring may not be well adapted in a changing environment.

Different reproductive strategies

Malarial parasite

The **plasmodium** is a **protist** that causes malaria. It can reproduce asexually in the human host but sexually in the mosquito.

Parasite enters human from mosquito bite

Parasite re-enters mosquito when it feeds

Keywords

Fusion ➤ Joining together; in biology the term is used to describe fertilisation

Internal fertilisation ➤ Gametes join **inside** the body of the female

External fertilisation ➤ Gametes join **outside** the body of the female

Aphid ➤ A type of sap-sucking insect

Strawberry plants and daffodils

These plants can reproduce sexually using flowers, or asexually using **runners** (strawberry) or **bulb division** (daffodils).

Strawberry plant

Runner

Daffodils

Bulb

Fungi

Many fungi, such as toadstools, mushrooms and moulds, can reproduce sexually (giving variation) or asexually by **spores**.

Mosquito

WS During your course, you will learn about historical developments in science and technology. It is important to appreciate how understanding develops from previous studies and their publication in scientific journals. Scientists build on each other's work and applications develop from this.

Malaria is a disease that kills many people every year. Treatment via anti-malarial drugs has been available for years and techniques are available to disrupt the parasite's life cycle. At the time of writing, scientists are close to developing a vaccine.

All these developments have come from an understanding of the complex interaction between the plasmodium and mosquito's life cycles. Studies were carried out by many different people and took about ten years to reach their conclusions. Finally, a Scottish physician called Sir Ronald Ross produced evidence for the complete life cycle of the malaria parasite in mosquitoes. For this work, he received the 1902 Nobel Prize in Medicine.

---

1. Sexual reproduction requires a greater devotion of resources by an organism. So why do so many organisms use it?
2. How do strawberry plants reproduce asexually?
3. State one advantage of asexual reproduction.

DNA

A cell

Nucleus

Chromosomes

DNA and the genome

The nucleus of each cell contains a complete set of genetic instructions called the **genetic code**. The information is carried as genes, which are small sections of DNA found on **chromosomes**. The genetic code controls cell activity and, consequently, characteristics of the whole organism.

A section of a chromosome

Gene

DNA double helix

DNA facts

➤ DNA is a **polymer**.

➤ It is made of two strands coiled around each other called a **double helix**.

➤ The genetic code is in the form of nitrogenous **bases**.

➤ Bases bond together in pairs forming **hydrogen bond** cross-links.

➤ The structure of DNA was discovered in 1953 by **James Watson** and **Francis Crick**, using experimental data from **Rosalind Franklin** and **Maurice Wilkins**.

➤ A single gene codes for a particular sequence of **amino acids**, which, in turn, makes up a single **protein**.

A section of the double helix

Bases

A — T

C — G

G — C

➤ Construct part of a DNA molecule using plasticine. Use different colours to represent bases, sugar and phosphate molecules. Use the model to illustrate how changes in the base sequence can result in new proteins. You could use different colours to represent different amino acids. Make appropriate shapes to represent each component. The diagrams used in this module are a good starting point.

➤ Use your model as a way of learning the names of the different components.

Keywords

Polymer ➤ A long chain molecule made up of individual units called **monomers**

Hydrogen bond ➤ A bond formed between hydrogen and oxygen atoms on different molecules close to each other

Anthropologists ➤ Scientists who study the human race and its evolution

The human genome

The **genome** of an organism is the entire genetic material present in an adult cell of an organism.

The Human Genome Project (HGP)

The HGP was an international study. Its purpose was to map the complete set of genes in the human body.

HGP scientists worked out the code of the human genome in three ways. They:

> determined the sequence of all the bases in the genome

> drew up maps showing the locations of the genes on chromosomes

> produced linkage maps that could be used for tracking inherited traits from generation to generation, e.g. for genetic diseases. This could then lead to targeted treatments for these conditions.

The results of the project, which involved collaboration between UK and US scientists, were published in 2003. Three billion base pairs were determined.

DNA structure and base sequences

The four bases in DNA are A, T, C and G. The code is 'read' on one strand of DNA. Three consecutive bases (a **triplet**) code for one particular amino acid. The sequence of these triplets determines the structure of a whole protein.

The bases are attached to a sugar phosphate **backbone**. These form a basic unit called a nucleotide.

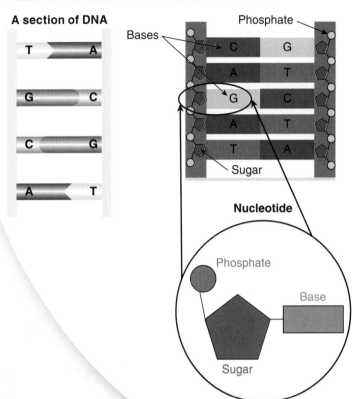

A section of DNA

Nucleotide

The mapping of the human genome has enabled anthropologists to work out historical human migration patterns. This has been achieved by collecting and analysing DNA samples from many people across the globe. The study is called the **Genographic Project**.

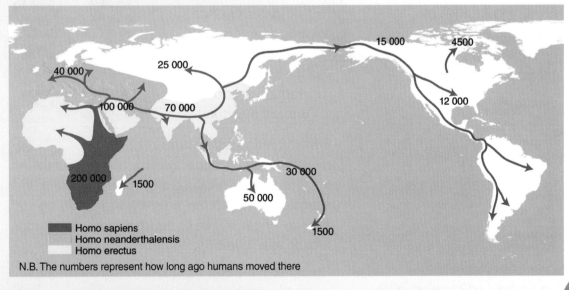

Homo sapiens
Homo neanderthalensis
Homo erectus

N.B. The numbers represent how long ago humans moved there

World map showing suggested migration patterns of early hominids

1. How has the Human Genome Project advanced medical science?
2. What do genes code for?

The genetic code

 DNA structure and base sequences

In **complementary strands** of DNA, T always bonds with A, and C with G.

Proteins are synthesised in structures called **ribosomes**, which are located in the cytoplasm of the cell. In order for the DNA code in the nucleus to be translated as new protein by the ribosomes, the following process occurs.

1. DNA unzips and exposes the bases on each strand.
2. A molecule of **messenger RNA** (**mRNA**) is constructed from one of these template strands.
3. The mRNA, which carries a complementary version of the gene, travels out of the nucleus to the ribosome in cytoplasm.
4. In the ribosome, the mRNA is 'read'. **Transfer RNA** (**tRNA**) molecules carry individual amino acids to add to a growing protein (**polypeptide**).
5. The new polypeptide folds into a unique shape and is released into the cytoplasm.

In the nucleus, **transcription** takes place.

In the ribosome, **translation** takes place.

The proteins that are produced carry out a specific function. Examples include enzymes, hormones or structural protein such as **collagen**.

Gene switching

Every cell contains a complete set of genes for the whole body, but only some of these genes are used in any one cell.

➤ Some genes are not **expressed**. They are said to be 'switched off'. Switching off genes is accomplished through **non-coding** DNA. Most DNA is non-coding.

➤ The genes that are 'switched on' eventually determine the function of a cell.

Mutations

Mutations (genetic variants):

➤ are changes to the structure of a DNA molecule

➤ occur continuously during the cell division process or as a result of external influences, e.g. exposure to radioactive materials or emissions such as X-rays or UV light

➤ usually have a neutral effect as amino acids may still be produced or the proteins produced work in the same way

➤ may result in harmful conditions or, more rarely, beneficial traits

➤ result in a change in base sequence and therefore changes in the amino acid sequence and protein structure.

3D view of protein

Normal gene | Mutated gene

The G base is substituted for an A base

Proteins produced as a result of mutation may no longer be able to carry out their function. This is because they have a different 3D structure. For example, an enzyme's active site may no longer fit with its substrate, or a structural protein may lose its strength.

Changes in the base sequence may be passed on to daughter cells when cell division occurs. This in turn may lead to offspring having genetic conditions.

Monohybrid crosses

Most characteristics or **traits** are the result of multiple alleles interacting but some are controlled by a single gene. Examples include fur colour in mice and the shape of ear lobes in humans. These genes exist as pairs called **alleles** on **homologous chromosomes**.

Alleles are described as being **dominant** or **recessive**.

➤ A **dominant** allele controls the development of a characteristic even if it is present on only one chromosome in a pair.

➤ A **recessive** allele controls the development of a characteristic only if a dominant allele is not present, i.e. if the recessive allele is present on both chromosomes in a pair.

Keywords

(HT) **Complementary strand** ➤ A sequence of bases that can bond with an equivalent sequence in DNA. Complementary strands can be DNA or mRNA

(HT) **Polypeptide** ➤ A sequence of peptides, which in turn are smaller chains of amino acids

(HT) **Transcription** ➤ Process by which a complementary strand of mRNA is made in the nucleus

(HT) **Translation** ➤ Process occurring in ribosomes where polypeptides are produced from the code in mRNA

Alleles ➤ Alternative forms of a gene on a homologous pair of chromosomes

Homologous chromosomes ➤ A pair of chromosomes carrying alleles that code for the same characteristics

Tongue rolling — T — Two dominant alleles, therefore can roll tongue. — T

Blue eyes — b — Brown is dominant, blue is recessive, therefore has brown eyes. — B — Brown eyes

Attached earlobes — e — No dominant alleles, both recessive, therefore has attached earlobes. — e — Attached earlobes

Homologous chromosomes

If **both chromosomes** in a pair contain the **same allele** of a gene, the individual is described as being **homozygous** for that gene or condition.

If the chromosomes in a pair contain **different alleles** of a gene, the individual is **heterozygous** for that gene or condition.

The combination of alleles for a particular characteristic is called the **genotype**. For example, the genotype for a homozygous dominant tongue-roller would be **TT**. The fact that this individual is able to roll their tongue is termed their **phenotype**.

Other examples are:

➤ **bb** (genotype), blue eyes (phenotype)

➤ **EE** or **Ee** (genotype), unattached/pendulous ear lobes (phenotype).

When a characteristic is determined by just one pair of alleles, as with eye colour and tongue rolling, it is called **monohybrid inheritance**.

(WS) During your course, you will be expected to recognise, draw and interpret scientific diagrams.

In this module, the way complementary strands of DNA are arranged can be worked out once you know that base T bonds with A and base C bonds with G.

Can you write out the complementary (DNA) strand to this sequence?

A T T A C G T G A G C C

(HT) **1.** How are the roles of tRNA and mRNA different from each other?

(HT) **2.** Describe the effects of incorrect base sequences on protein manufacture.

31

Inheritance and genetic disorders

Genetic diagrams

Genetic diagrams are used to show all the possible combinations of alleles and outcomes for a particular gene. They use:

➤ capital letters for dominant alleles
➤ lower-case letters for recessive alleles.

For eye colour, brown is dominant and blue is recessive. So B represents a brown allele and b represents a blue allele.

Example 1

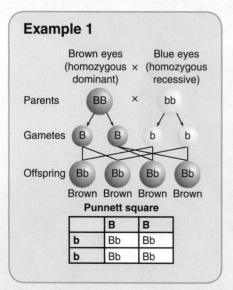

	B	B
b	Bb	Bb
b	Bb	Bb

Example 2

	B	b
B	BB	Bb
b	Bb	bb

Example 3

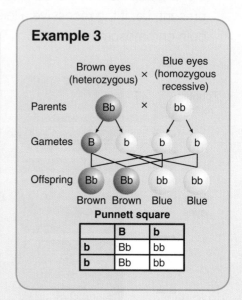

	B	b
b	Bb	bb
b	Bb	bb

WS You need to be able to interpret genetic diagrams and work out ratios of offspring.

➤ In Example 2 above, the phenotypes of the offspring are 'brown eyes' and 'blue eyes'. As there are potentially three times as many brown-eyed children as blue-eyed, the phenotypes are said to be in a 3:1 ratio.

➤ In Example 3 above, the ratio would be 1:1 because half of the theoretical offspring are brown-eyed and half blue-eyed. Another way of saying this is that the probability of parents producing a brown-eyed child is 50%, or ½, or 0.5.

Most traits result not from one pair of alleles but from multiple genes interacting, e.g. inheritance of blood groups in the **ABO** system.

HT In exams, you may be asked to construct your own punnett squares to solve genetic cross problems like the ones above.

Family trees

Family trees are another way of showing how genetic traits can be passed on. Here is an example.

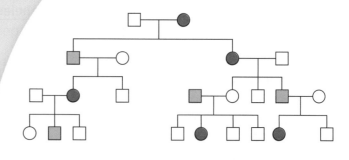

Key:	☐ Male
	○ Female
	■ Male with trait
	● Female with trait

Inheritance of sex

Sex in humans/mammals is determined by whole chromosomes. These are the 23rd pair and are called sex chromosomes. There is an 'X' chromosome and a smaller 'Y' chromosome. The other 22 chromosome pairs carry the remainder of genes coding for the rest of the body's characteristics.

All egg cells carry X chromosomes. Half the sperm carry X chromosomes and half carry Y chromosomes. The sex of an individual depends on whether the egg is fertilised by an X-carrying sperm or a Y-carrying sperm.

If an X sperm fertilises the egg it will become a girl. If a Y sperm fertilises the egg it will become a boy. The chances of these events are equal, which results in approximately equal numbers of male and female offspring.

Inherited diseases

Some disorders are caused by a 'faulty' gene, which means they can be **inherited**. One example is **polydactyly**, which is caused by a dominant allele and results in extra fingers or toes. The condition is not life-threatening.

Cystic fibrosis, on the other hand, can limit life expectancy. It causes the mucus in respiratory passages and the gut lining to be very thick, leading to build-up of phlegm and difficulty in producing correct digestive enzymes.

Cystic fibrosis is caused by a recessive allele. This means that an individual will only exhibit symptoms if both recessive alleles are present in the genotype. Those carrying just one allele will not show symptoms, but could potentially pass the condition on to offspring. Such people are called **carriers**.

Conditions such as cystic fibrosis are mostly caused by **faulty alleles** that are **recessive**.

Knowing that there is a 1 in 4 chance that their child might have cystic fibrosis gives parents the opportunity to make decisions about whether to take the risk and have a child. This is a very difficult decision to make.

Technology has advanced and it is now possible to screen embryos for genetic disorders.

➤ If an embryo has a life-threatening condition it could be destroyed, or simply not be implanted if IVF was being applied.

➤ Alternatively, new gene therapy techniques might be able to reverse the effects of the condition, resulting in a healthy baby.

As yet, these possibilities have to gain approval from ethics committees – some people think that this type of 'interference with nature' could have harmful consequences.

1. If a homozygous brown-eyed individual is crossed with a homozygous blue-eyed individual, what is the probability of them producing a blue-eyed child?
2. What is the genotype of a human female?
3. How does the combination of two faulty, cystic fibrosis genes affect the phenotype of the person who possesses them?

Variation and evolution

32

Keywords

Anatomy ➤ The study of structures within the bodies of organisms

Vertebrate ➤ Animal with a backbone

Compress ➤ Squash or squeeze. In geology, this is usually due to Earth movements or laying down sediments

Extinction ➤ When there are no more members of a species left living

Variation

The two major factors that contribute to the appearance and function of an organism are:

➤ **genetic information** passed on from parents to offspring

➤ **environment** – the conditions that affect that organism during its lifetime, e.g. climate, diet, etc.

These two factors account for the large variation we see **within** and **between** species. In most cases, both of these factors play a part.

Evolution

Put simply, evolution is the theory that all organisms have arisen from simpler life forms over billions of years. It is driven by the **mechanism** of **natural selection**. For natural selection to occur, there must be genetic variation between individuals of the same species. This is caused by mutation or new combinations of genes resulting from sexual reproduction (see Module 30).

Most mutations have no effect on the phenotype of an organism. Where they do, and if the environment is changing, this can lead to relatively rapid change.

Evidence for evolution

Evidence for evolution comes from many sources. It includes:

➤ comparing genomes of different organisms

➤ studying embryos and their similarities

➤ looking at changes in species during modern times, e.g. antibiotic resistance in bacteria

➤ comparing the **anatomy** of different forms

➤ the fossil record.

One of the earliest sources of evidence for evolution was the discovery of fossils.

Further evidence for evolution – the pentadactyl limb

If you compare the forelimbs of a variety of **vertebrates**, you can see that the bone structures are all variations on a five-digit form, whether it be a leg, a wing or a flipper. This suggests that there was a common ancestral form from which these organisms developed.

Human   Cow   Horse   Whale   Bird

How fossils are formed

1 When an animal or plant dies, the processes of decay usually cause all the body tissues to break down. In rare circumstances, the organism's body is rapidly **covered** and oxygen is prevented from reaching it. Instead of decay, fossilisation occurs.

2 Over hundreds of thousands of years, further sediments are laid down and **compress** the organism's remains.

3 Parts of the organism, such as bones and teeth, are **replaced by minerals** from solutions in the rock.

4 Earth upheavals, e.g. **tectonic plate movement**, bring sediments containing the fossils nearer the Earth's surface.

5 Erosion of the rock by wind, rain and rivers exposes the fossil. At this stage, the remains might be found and excavated by **paleontologists**.

Fossils can also be formed from footprints, burrows and traces of tree roots.

By comparing different fossils and where they are found in the rock layers, paleontologists can gain insights into how one form may have developed into another.

Difficulties occur with earlier life forms because many were **soft-bodied** and therefore not as well-preserved as organisms with bones or shells. Any that *are* formed are easily destroyed by Earth movements. As a result of this, scientists cannot be certain about exactly how life began.

Extinction

The fossil record provides evidence that most organisms that once existed have become **extinct**. In fact, there have been at least five **mass extinctions** in geological history where most organisms died out. One of these coincides with the disappearance of dinosaurs.

Causes of extinction include:
➤ **catastrophic events**, e.g. volcanic eruptions, asteroid collisions
➤ changes to the environment over geological time
➤ new **predators**
➤ new **diseases**
➤ new, more successful **competitors**.

Use different-coloured pieces of card to depict one of the ideas covered in this module. Keep the design simple.
For example, you could:
➤ show different forms of the pentadactyl limb and how they have evolved from a common ancestor
➤ produce five scenes showing the different stages of fossilisation.
When you have completed your design, explain the process/idea to a revision buddy.

1. State two pieces of evidence that support the theory of evolution through natural selection.
2. Why are fossils so rare?

Darwin and evolution

33

Keywords

Fittest ➤ The most adapted individual or species
Competition ➤ When two individuals or populations seek to exploit a resource, e.g. food. One individual/population will eventually replace the other

Human evolution

Modern man has evolved from a common ancestor that gave rise to all the primates: gorillas, chimpanzees and orangutans. DNA comparisons have shown we are most closely related to the chimpanzee.

The evolution of man can be traced back over the last four to five million years. Over this period of time, the **human form** (hominid) has developed:

➤ a more upright, bipedal stance
➤ less body hair
➤ a smaller and less 'domed' forehead
➤ greater intelligence and use of tools, initially from stone. These tools can be dated using scientific techniques, e.g. radiometric dating and carbon dating.

There have been significant finds of fossils that give clues to human evolution.

1 **Ardi** – at 4.4 million years old, this is the oldest, most complete hominid skeleton.

2 **Lucy** – from 3.2 million years ago, this is one of the first fossils to show an upright walking stance.

3 **Proconsul skull** – discovered by **Mary Leakey** and her husband; the hominid is thought to be from about 1.6 million years ago.

Darwin's theory of evolution through natural selection

Within a population of organisms there is a range of variation among individuals. This is caused by genes. Some differences will be beneficial; some will not.

Charles Darwin

Beneficial characteristics make an organism more likely to survive and pass on their genes to the next generation. This is especially true if the environment is changing. This ability to be successful is called **survival of the fittest**.

Species that are not well adapted to their environment may become extinct. This process of change is summed up in the theory of evolution through **natural selection**, put forward by **Charles Darwin** in the nineteenth century.

Many theories have tried to explain how life might have come about in its present form.

However, Darwin's theory is accepted by most scientists today. This is because it explains a wide range of observations and has been discussed and tested by many scientists.

Darwin's theory can be reduced to five ideas. They are:

➤ variation
➤ survival of the fittest
➤ competition
➤ inheritance
➤ extinction.

This activity should help you memorise Darwin's theory and learn how to apply the features using different scenarios.

➤ Arrange pieces of coloured paper into sets of five. About three lots will do – so fifteen altogether.
➤ On each set, write out the headings for the theory of evolution through natural selection: variation, competition, survival of the fittest, inheritance and extinction.
➤ Now research three case studies relating to natural selection, e.g. warfarin resistance in rats or the shape of shells in Galapagos tortoises. As you read, write down information on each of the five cards.

Darwin's ideas are illustrated in the following two examples.

Example 1: peppered moths

Variation – most peppered moths are pale and speckled. They are easily camouflaged amongst the lichens on silver birch tree bark. There are some rare, dark-coloured varieties (that originally arose from genetic mutation). They are easily seen and eaten by birds.

Competition – in areas with high levels of air pollution, lichens die and the bark becomes discoloured by soot. The lighter peppered moths are now put at a competitive disadvantage.

Survival of the fittest – the dark (melanic) moths are now more likely to avoid detection by pedators.

Inheritance – the genes for dark colour are passed on to offspring and gradually become more common in the general population.

Extinction – if the environment remains polluted, the lighter form is more likely to become extinct.

Dark peppered moth

Peppered moth

Example 2: methicillin-resistant bacteria

The resistance of some bacteria to antibiotics is an increasing problem. MRSA bacteria have become more common in hospital wards and are difficult to eradicate.

Variation – bacteria mutate by chance, giving them a resistance to antibiotics.

Competition – the non-resistant bacteria are more likely to be killed by the antibiotic and become less competitive.

Survival of the fittest – the antibiotic-resistant bacteria survive and reproduce more often.

Inheritance – resistant bacteria pass on their genes to a new generation; the gene becomes more common in the general population.

Extinction – non-resistant bacteria are replaced by the newer, resistant strain.

To slow down the rate at which new, resistant strains of bacteria can develop:
➤ doctors are urged not to prescribe antibiotics for obvious viral infections or for mild bacterial infections
➤ patients should complete the full course of antibiotics to ensure that **all** bacteria are destroyed (so that none will survive to mutate into resistant strains).

Species become more and more specialised as they evolve and adapt to their environmental conditions.

The point at which a new species is formed occurs when the original population can no longer interbreed with the newer, 'mutant' population. For this to occur, **isolation** needs to happen.

Speciation
➤ Groups of the same species that are separated from each other by physical boundaries (like mountains or seas) will not be able to breed and share their genes. This is called **geographical isolation**.
➤ Over long periods of time, separate groups may specialise so much that they cannot successfully breed any longer and so two new species are formed – this is **reproductive isolation**.

1. Define evolution and natural selection.
2. State two examples where natural selection has been observed by scientists in recent times.
3. What has to happen to the beneficial genes for a helpful phenotype to spread through a population?

The pioneers of evolution

Charles Darwin published his findings and theories in a book called *On the Origin of Species* (1859). At the time, the reaction to Darwin's theory, particularly from religious authorities, was hostile. They felt he was saying that 'people were descended from monkeys' (although he wasn't) and that he denied God's role in the creation of man. This meant that Darwin's theory was only slowly and reluctantly accepted by many people in spite of his many eminent supporters. In Darwin's time there wasn't the wealth of evidence we have today from the study of genetics and DNA. (The structure of DNA wasn't made plain until 1953.)

Jean-Baptiste Lamarck had published ideas about the gradual change in organisms before Darwin but he put forward a different approach (now known to be inaccurate). He believed that evolution was driven by the inheritance of acquired characteristics. However, he thought that:

➤ organisms changed during their lifetime as they struggled to survive
➤ these changes were passed on to the offspring.

For example, he said that when giraffes stretched their necks to reach leaves higher up, this extra neck length was passed on to their offspring.

Lamarck's theory was rejected because there was no evidence that the changes occurring in an individual's lifetime could alter their genes and so be passed on to their offspring. The difference between Darwin and Lamarck's approach is shown in the picture.

Lamarck believed that the necks of giraffes stretched during their lifetime to reach food in trees. They then passed this characteristic on to the next generation.

Darwin believed giraffes that had longer necks could reach more food in trees, so they were more likely to survive and reproduce (survival of the fittest).

Alfred Russel Wallace also put forward a theory of evolution by natural selection. In fact, he and Darwin jointly published writings a year before Darwin's *On the Origin of Species*.

Wallace gathered evidence from around the world to back up the theory of natural selection. In particular, he looked at how speciation could occur and wrote extensively about warning colouration in animals.

Evolution – the modern synthesis

Gregor Mendel carried out breeding programmes for plants in the middle of the nineteenth century. He discovered that characteristics could be passed down as 'units' (which we now know as genes) in a predictable way.

HT **WS** The significance of Mendel's work was only realised after his death. This shows the importance of a scientist's work being published so that others can build on it. It also shows that, sometimes, apparently trivial phenomena and their study can lead to important theories. In this way, our understanding of the world we live in is enhanced.

In your course, you will need to give examples of **how a model can be tested** by **observation** and **experiment**. Mendel's work is a classic example of this because he could show that the ratios of offspring in his pea plant experiments could be accurately predicted.

Other evidence to support the theory of natural selection

Since the nineteenth century, a sequence of findings and techniques has further reinforced our ideas about evolution by natural selection.

➤ In the late nineteenth century, chromosomes were observed during cell division under the microscope.
➤ In the early twentieth century, the link between Mendel's 'units' and genes was made. The idea that genes were found on chromosomes was put forward.
➤ In the mid-twentieth century, the structure of DNA was worked out by Watson and Crick.

Cloning

Studies of genetics have led to many technological advancements. One of these is the ability to **clone** cells, organs or even whole organisms.

Keywords

Clone ➤ A genetically identical cell, tissue, organ or organism

Surrogate mother ➤ An adult female animal that has had an embryo implanted into her uterus. The surrogate gives birth to the offspring but has no genetic relationship to it

Cuttings

When a gardener has a plant with all the desired characteristics, he/she may choose to produce lots of them by taking stem, leaf or root cuttings. The cuttings are grown in a damp atmosphere until roots develop.

Cloning by tissue culture

To mass-produce plants that are genetically identical to the parent plant and to each other, horticulturalists follow this method.

1. Select a parent plant with the characteristics that you want.
2. Scrape off lots of small pieces of tissue into several beakers containing nutrients and hormones.
3. A week or two later there will be lots of genetically identical plantlets growing.
4. Repeat the process.

Embryo transplantation

Embryo transplantation is now commonly used to breed farm animals.

1. Sperm is collected from an adult male with desirable characteristics.
2. A selected female is artificially inseminated with the male animal's sperm.
3. The fertilised egg develops into an embryo that is removed from the mother at an early stage.
4. In the laboratory, the embryo is split to form several clones.
5. Each clone is transplanted into a female who will be the **surrogate mother** to the new calf.

Adult cell cloning

1. The diploid nucleus is taken from a mature cell (ordinary body cell) of the donor organism.
2. The diploid nucleus, containing all of the donor's genetic information, is inserted into an empty egg cell (i.e. an egg cell with the nucleus removed or enucleated). This is nuclear transfer. A tiny electric shock is applied at this stage to trigger cell division in the embryo.
3. The egg cell, containing the diploid nucleus, is stimulated so that it begins to divide by mitosis.
4. The resulting embryo is implanted in the uterus of a 'surrogate mother'.
5. The embryo develops into a foetus and is born as normal.

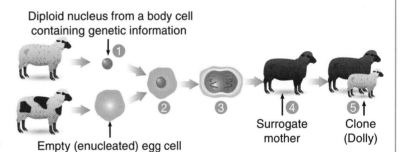

Diploid nucleus from a body cell containing genetic information

Empty (enucleated) egg cell

Surrogate mother

Clone (Dolly)

1. How did Darwin's mechanism of natural selection differ from Lamarck's?
2. How did Mendel's work provide further evidence for Darwin's theory?
3. What is the advantage of cloning plants or animals?

Selective breeding and genetic engineering

Keywords

Herbicide ➤ A chemical applied to crops to kill weeds

HT Vector ➤ Organism, cell or molecule that can be used to transfer DNA from one organism to another

HT Plasmid ➤ A ring of DNA found in bacteria

Selective breeding

Farmers and dog breeders have used the principles of selective breeding for thousands of years by keeping the best animals and plants for breeding.

For example, to breed Dalmatian dogs, the spottiest dogs have been bred through the generations to eventually get Dalmatians. The factor most affected by selective breeding in dogs is probably temperament. Most breeds are either naturally obedient to humans or are trained to be so.

This is the process of selective breeding.

Select the desired characteristics in parents. ➤ Allow the individuals to breed (or cross-pollinate if you are dealing with plants). ➤ Select the desired offspring and allow them to become parents of the next generation.

This process has to be repeated many times to get the desired results.

Advantages of selective breeding
➤ It results in an organism with the 'right' characteristics for a particular function.
➤ In farming and horticulture, it is a more efficient and economically viable process than natural selection.

Disadvantages of selective breeding
➤ Intensive selective breeding reduces the gene pool – the range of alleles in the population decreases so there is **less variation**.
➤ Lower variation reduces a species' ability to respond to environmental change.
➤ It can lead to an accumulation of harmful recessive characteristics (in-breeding), e.g. restriction of respiratory pathways and dislocatable joints in bulldogs.

Examples of selective breeding

Modern food plants

Three of our modern vegetables have come from a single ancestor by selective breeding. (Remember, it can take many, many generations to get the desired results.)

Cabbage (large bud) Brussel sprouts (many small buds) Cauliflower (large flower head)

Selective breeding in plants has also been undertaken to produce:
➤ disease resistance in crops
➤ large, unusual flowers in garden plants.

Modern cattle

Selective breeding can contribute to improved yields in cattle. Here are some examples.

➤ **Quantity of milk** – years of selecting and breeding cattle that produce larger than average quantities of milk has produced herds of cows that produce high daily volumes of milk.

➤ **Quality of milk** – as a result of selective breeding, Jersey cows produce milk that is rich and creamy, and can therefore be sold at a higher price.

➤ **Beef production** – the characteristics of the Hereford and Angus varieties have been selected for beef production over the past 200 years or more. They include hardiness, early maturity, high numbers of offspring and the swift, efficient conversion of grass into body mass (meat).

Genetic engineering

All living organisms use the same basic genetic code (DNA). So genes can be transferred from one organism to another in order to deliberately change the recipient's characteristics. This process is called genetic engineering or genetic modification (GM).

Altering the genetic make-up of an organism can be done for many reasons.

➤ **To improve resistance to** herbicides: for example, soya plants are genetically modified by inserting a gene that makes them resistant to a herbicide. When the crop fields are sprayed with the herbicide only the weeds die, leaving the soya plants without competition so they can grow better. Resistance to frost or disease can also be genetically engineered. Bigger yields result.

➤ **To improve the quality of food**: for example, bigger and more tasty fruit.

➤ **To produce a substance you require**: for example, the gene for human insulin can be inserted into bacteria or fungi, to make human insulin on a large scale to treat diabetes.

➤ **Disease resistance**: crop plants receive genes that give them resistance to the bacterium *Bacillus thuringiensis*.

Advantages of genetic engineering
➤ It allows organisms with new features to be produced rapidly.
➤ It can be used to make biochemical processes cheaper and more efficient.
➤ In the future, it may be possible to use genetic engineering to change a person's genes and cure certain disorders, e.g. cystic fibrosis. This is an area of research called gene therapy.

Disadvantages of genetic engineering
➤ Transplanted genes may have unexpected harmful effects on human health.
➤ Some people are worried that GM plants may cross-breed with wild plants and release their new genes into the environment.

HT Producing insulin

The following method is used to produce insulin.

1. The human gene for insulin production is identified and removed using a **restriction enzyme**, which cuts through the DNA strands in precise places.
2. The same restriction enzyme is used to cut open a ring of bacterial **vector** DNA (a **plasmid**).
3. Other enzymes called **ligases** are then used to insert the section of human DNA into the plasmid. The DNA can be 'spliced' in this way because the ends of the strands are 'sticky'.
4. The plasmid is reinserted into a bacterium, which starts to divide rapidly. As it divides, it replicates the plasmid.
5. The bacteria are cultivated on a large scale in fermenters. Each bacterium carries the instructions to make insulin. When the bacteria make the protein, commercial quantities of insulin are produced.

Part of a human DNA strand

Desired gene

Desired gene isolated

Desired gene inserted into target DNA

Target bacterium replicates itself

Bacterium

Sometimes, other vectors are used to introduce human DNA into organisms, e.g. viruses. It is important that the hybrid genes are transferred to the host organism at an early stage of its development, e.g. the egg or the embryo stage. As the cells are quite undifferentiated, the desired characteristics from the inserted DNA are more likely to develop.

Design a poster describing the stages of selective breeding.

1. What advantages does genetic engineering have over selective breeding?
2. Should we be expanding the range of GM foods we eat? Give one reason **for** this proposal and one reason **against**.

35

There is a huge variety of living organisms. Scientists group or classify them using shared characteristics. This is important because it helps to:

➤ work out how organisms evolved on Earth
➤ understand how organisms coexist in ecological communities
➤ identify and monitor rare organisms that are at risk from extinction.

Classification

Carl Linnaeus

The origins of classification

In the past, observable characteristics were used to place organisms into categories.

In the eighteenth century, **Carl Linnaeus** produced the first classification system. He developed a hierarchical arrangement where larger groups were subdivided into smaller ones.

Kingdom	Largest group
Phylum	
Class	
Order	
Family	
Genus	
Species	Smallest group

Linnaeus also developed a **binomial system** for naming organisms according to their genus and species. For example, the common domestic cat is *Felis catus*. Its full classification would be:

➤ Kingdom: *Animalia*
➤ Phylum: *Chordata*
➤ Class: *Mammalia*
➤ Order: *Carnivora*
➤ Family: *Felidae*
➤ Genus: *Felis*
➤ Species: *Catus*.

Linnaeus' system was built on and resulted in a **five-kingdom system**. Developments that contributed to the introduction of this system included improvements in microscopes and a more thorough understanding of the biochemical processes that occur in all living things. For example, the presence of particular chemical pathways in a range of organisms indicated that they probably had a **common ancestor** and so were more closely related than organisms that didn't share these pathways.

Kingdom	Features	Examples
Plants	Cellulose cell wall Use light energy to produce food	Flowering plants Trees Ferns Mosses
Animals	Multicellular Feed on other organisms	Vertebrates Invertebrates
Fungi	Cell wall of chitin Produce spores	Toadstools Mushrooms Yeasts Moulds
Protoctista Protozoa	Mostly single-celled organisms	Amoeba Paramecium
Prokaryotes	No nucleus	Bacteria Blue–green algae

Keywords

Binomial system ➤ 'Two name' system of naming species using Latin

Common ancestor ➤ Organism that gave rise to two different branches of organisms in an evolutionary tree

The classification diagram below illustrates how different lines of evidence can be used. The classes of vertebrates share a common ancestor and so are quite closely related. Evidence for this lies in comparative anatomy (e.g. the pentadactyl limb) and similarities in biochemical pathways.

Vertebrates

In more recent times, improvements in science have led to a **three-domain system** developed by **Carl Woese**. In this system organisms are split into:

➤ **archaea** (primitive bacteria)
➤ **bacteria** (true bacteria)
➤ **eukaryota** (including Protista, fungi, plants and animals).

Further improvements in science include chemical analysis and further refinements in comparisons between non-coding sections of DNA.

Evolutionary trees

Tree diagrams are useful for depicting relationships between similar groups of organisms and determining how they may have developed from common ancestors. Fossil evidence can be invaluable in establishing these relationships.

Here, two species are shown to have evolved from a common ancestor.

Common ancestor

WS You need to understand how new evidence and data leads to changes in models and theories.

In the case of the three-domain system, a more accurate and cohesive classification structure was proposed as a result of improvements in microscopy and increasing knowledge of organisms' internal structures.

These apes share a common ancestor

1. What do the first and second words in the binomial name of an organism mean?
2. Name four groups of organisms found in the domain *Eukaryota*.
3. It is thought that chimpanzees and humans evolved from a now extinct ape. What term describes this animal?

Mind map

Cuttings

Embryo transplantation

Other evidence to support natural selection

Tissue culture

Modern food plants

Fungi

Strawberry plants and daffodils

Asexual reproduction

Modern cattle

Different reproductive strategies

Malarial parasite

Cloning

Examples

Pioneers of evolution

Producing insulin

Adult cell cloning

Genetic engineering

Reproduction

Evolution – the modern synthesis

Selective breeding

Sexual reproduction

Selective breeding and genetic engineering

Penicillin-resistant bacteria

Evolutionary trees

Peppered moths

Classification

Darwin's theory

Speciation

INHERITANCE, VARIATION AND EVOLUTION

The origins of classification

Darwin and evolution

Human evolution

Evidence for evolution

Evolution

Inheritance and genetic disorders

Inherited diseases

Variation

Inheritance of sex

Family trees

Genetic diagrams

Variation and evolution

How fossils are formed

Mutations

The genetic code

Gene switching

Pentadactyl limb

Extinction

DNA structure and base sequences

Monohybrid crosses

DNA

DNA and the genome

DNA facts

DNA structure and base sequences

The human genome

The HGP

Practice questions

1. Scientists believe that the whale may have evolved from a horse-like ancestor that lived in swampy regions millions of years ago. Suggest how whales could have evolved from a horse-like mammal. In your answer, use Darwin's theory of natural selection. **(4 marks)**

2. The diagram below shows the inheritance of cystic fibrosis in a family.

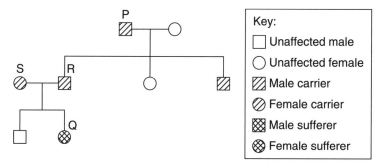

Key:
☐ Unaffected male
○ Unaffected female
▨ Male carrier
⊘ Female carrier
▨ Male sufferer
⊗ Female sufferer

Cystic fibrosis is caused by a recessive allele, f. The dominant allele of the gene is represented by F.

a) Give the alleles for person P. **(1 mark)**

b) Give the alleles for person Q. **(1 mark)**

3. The schematic below shows how insulin can be genetically engineered.

1. Human gene removed using an enzyme

2. Plasmid in bacterium is cut open using enzymes

3.

4. Plasmid reinserted into bacterium

5.

a) Write the missing steps **3** and **5**. **(2 marks)**

b) Name the type of enzyme used in steps **1** and **2**. **(1 mark)**

4. The diagram shows a molecule of DNA.

X

a) Name the part labelled **X** in the DNA diagram. **(1 mark)**

b) The 'backbone' of the molecule is arranged in such a way as to make it very stable. Name the term used to describe the shape of DNA. **(1 mark)**

Keyword

Environmental resources ➤ Materials or factors that organisms need to survive, e.g. high oxygen concentration, living space or a particular food supply

Communities

Ecosystems are physical environments with a particular set of conditions (**abiotic** factors), plus all the organisms that live in them. The organisms interact through competition and predation. An ecosystem can support itself without any influx of other factors or materials. Its energy source (usually the Sun) is the only external factor.

Other terms help to describe aspects of the environment.

➤ The **habitat** of an animal or plant is the part of the physical environment where it lives. There are many types of habitat, each with particular characteristics, e.g. pond, hedgerow, coral reef.

➤ A **population** is the number of individuals of a species in a defined area.

➤ A **community** is the total number of individuals of all the different populations of organisms that live together in a habitat at any one time.

An organism must be well-suited to its habitat to be able to compete with other species for limited **environmental resources**. Even organisms within the same species may compete in order to survive and breed. Organisms that are specialised in this way are restricted to that type of habitat because their adaptations are unsuitable elsewhere.

Resources that plants compete over include:
➤ light
➤ space
➤ water
➤ minerals.

Animals compete over:
➤ food
➤ mates.
➤ territory.

Interdependence

In communities, each species may depend on other species for food, shelter, pollination and seed dispersal. If one species is removed, it may have knock-on effects for other species.

Stable communities contain species whose numbers fluctuate very little over time. The populations are in balance with the physical factors that exist in that habitat. Stable communities include **tropical rainforests** and ancient oak **woodlands**.

Adaptations

Adaptations:
➤ are special features or behaviours that make an organism particularly well-suited to its environment and better able to compete with other organisms for limited resources
➤ can be thought of as a biological solution to an environmental challenge – evolution provides the solution and makes species fit their environment.

Animals have developed in many different ways to become well adapted to their environment and to help them survive. Adaptations are usually of three types:

➤ **Structural** – for example, skin colouration in chameleons provides camouflage to hide them from predators.
➤ **Functional** – for example, some worms have blood with a high affinity for oxygen; this helps them to survive in anaerobic environments.
➤ **Behavioural** – for example, penguins huddle together to conserve body heat in the Antarctic habitat.

Look at the **polar bear** and its life in a very cold climate. It has:

➤ small ears and large bulk to reduce its surface area to volume ratio and so reduce heat loss
➤ a large amount of insulating fat (blubber)
➤ thick white fur for insulation and camouflage
➤ large feet to spread its weight on snow and ice
➤ fur on the soles of its paws for insulation and grip
➤ powerful legs so it is a good swimmer and runner, which enables it to catch its food
➤ sharp claws and teeth to capture prey.

The **cactus** is well adapted to living in a desert habitat. It:

➤ has a rounded shape, which gives a small surface area to volume ratio and therefore reduces water loss
➤ has a thick waxy cuticle to reduce water loss
➤ stores water in a spongy layer inside its stem to resist drought
➤ has sunken stomata, meaning that air movement is reduced, minimising loss of water vapour through them
➤ has leaves that take the form of spines to reduce water loss and to protect the cactus from predators.

Some organisms have biochemical adaptations. **Extremophiles** can survive extreme environmental conditions. For example:

➤ bacteria living in deep sea vents have optimum temperatures for enzymes that are much higher than 37°C
➤ icefish have antifreeze chemicals in their bodies, which lower the freezing point of body fluids
➤ some organisms can resist high salt concentrations or pressure.

WS During your course you will be asked to suggest explanations for observations made in the field or laboratory. These include:

➤ suggesting factors for which organisms are competing in a certain habitat
➤ giving possible adaptations for organisms in a habitat.

For example, low-lying plants in forest ecosystems often have specific adaptations for maximising light absorption as they are shaded by taller plants. Adaptations might include leaves with a large surface area and higher concentrations of photosynthetic pigments to absorb the correct wavelengths and lower intensities of light.

1. How is an ecosystem different from a habitat?
2. Which is the more stable community – a mixed-leaf woodland or a dry river bed in Africa? What is the reason for this?
3. How is a community different from a population?
4. Give two examples of extremophiles.
5. Why is it important for organisms to be well adapted?

Studying ecosystems 1

Keyword

Sample ➤ A small area or population that is measured to give an indication of numbers within a larger area or population

Testing soil pH

Taking measurements in ecosystems

Ecosystems involve the interaction between **non-living** (**abiotic**) and **living** (**biotic**) parts of the environment. So it is important to identify which factors need to be measured in a particular habitat.

Abiotic factors include:
➤ light intensity
➤ temperature
➤ moisture levels
➤ soil pH and mineral content
➤ wind intensity and direction
➤ carbon dioxide levels for plants
➤ oxygen levels for aquatic animals.

Biotic factors include:
➤ availability of food
➤ new predators arriving
➤ new pathogens
➤ one species out-competing another.

Measuring biotic factors – sampling methods

It is usually impossible to count all the species living in a particular area, so a **sample** is taken.

When sampling, make sure you:
➤ **take a big enough sample** to make the estimate good and reliable – the larger the sample, the more accurate the results.
➤ **sample randomly** – the more random the sample, the more likely it is to be representative of the population.

Design a poster showing the different sampling methods.

Quadrats

Quadrats are square frames that typically have sides of length 0.5 m. They provide excellent results as long as they are placed randomly. The population of a certain species can then be estimated.

For example, if an average of 4 dandelion plants are found in a 0.25 m² quadrat, a scientist would estimate that 16 dandelion plants would be found in each 1 m² and 16 000 dandelion plants in a 1000 m² field.

A quadrat
0.5 m
Area = 0.25 m²
0.5 m

Transects

Sometimes an environmental scientist may want to look at how species change across a habitat, or the boundary between two different habitats – for example, the plants found in a field as you move away from a hedgerow.

This needs a different approach that is systematic rather than random.

1. Lay down a line such as a tape measure. Mark regular intervals on it.
2. Next to the line, lay down a small quadrat. Estimate or count the number of plants of the different species. This can sometimes be done by estimating the percentage cover.
3. Move the quadrat along at regular intervals. Estimate and record the plant populations at each point until the end of the line.

Repeated transects

Hedge

5 m intervals

Sampling methods

Sampling animal populations is more problematic as they are mobile and well adapted to evade capture. Here are four of the main techniques used.

Pooters

Insects sucked in here | You suck here
Fine mesh to stop you from sucking the insects into your mouth

This is a simple technique in which insects are gathered up easily without harm. With this method, you get to find out which species are actually present, although you have to be systematic about your sampling in order to get representative results and it is difficult to get ideas of numbers.

Sweepnets

Sweepnets are used in long grass or moderately dense woodland where there are lots of shrubs. Again, it is difficult to get truly representative samples, particularly in terms of the relative numbers of organisms.

Pitfall traps

Pitfall traps are set into the ground and used to catch small insects, e.g. beetles. Sometimes a mixture of ethanol or detergent and water is placed in the bottom of the trap to kill the samples, and prevent them from escaping. This method can give an indication of the relative numbers of organisms in a given area if enough traps are used to give a representative sample.

Capture/recapture

The capture/recapture method is sometimes called the **Lincoln index**.

1. Animals are caught humanely – for example, woodlice are caught in traps overnight. Their number is counted and recorded.
2. The animals are marked in some way – for example, water boatmen (a type of insect) can be marked with a drop of waterproof paint on their upper surface.
3. The marked animals are then released back into the population for a suitable amount of time.
4. A second sample is obtained, which will contain some marked animals and some unmarked. The numbers in each group are again counted.

Certain assumptions are made when using capture/recapture data. These include:

➤ no death, immigration or emigration
➤ each sample being collected in exactly the same way without bias
➤ the marks given to the animals not affecting their survival rate, e.g. using paint on invertebrates requires care because if too much is added it can enter their respiratory passages and kill them.

The following formula can then be used to estimate the total population size in the habitat.

$$\text{population size} = \frac{\text{number in first sample (all marked)} \times \text{number in second sample (marked and unmarked)}}{\text{number in second sample that were previously marked}}$$

Example

Fifty-six mice are caught in woodland and a small section of fur removed from their tail with clippers. The mice are released. The next evening, a further sample of sixty-two mice are caught. Twenty-five of these mice have shaved tails. What is the total population size?

$$\text{Population size} = \frac{56 \times 62}{25} = 139 \text{ mice}$$

Keys

Correctly identifying species in a sample can be difficult. Using keys like this one can help to identify organisms.

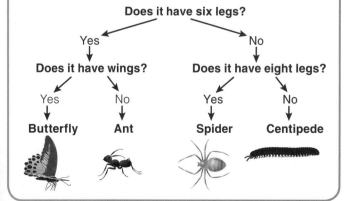

Does it have six legs?
Yes → Does it have wings?
No → Does it have eight legs?
Does it have wings? Yes → Butterfly, No → Ant
Does it have eight legs? Yes → Spider, No → Centipede

1. In what situation would you use a transect? What information would it give you?

Studying ecosystems 2

Keyword

Indicator species ➤ Organism used as an indicator of pollution

Measuring abiotic factors

Many measurements connected with climate and the weather can be measured using meteorological equipment. Measuring chemical pollutant levels is particularly useful as they give information about concentrations of pollutants. This can be done by **direct chemical tests**.

For example, water can be tested for pH and samples can be assessed for metal ion content, e.g. mercury.

Indicator species

The occurrence of certain **indicator species** can be observed by sampling an area and noting whether the species is present or not, together with the overall numbers of the species. For example, insect larvae and other invertebrates can act as an indicator of water pollution. When sewage works outflow into a stream, this pollutes the water by altering the levels of nitrogen compounds in the stream and reducing oxygen levels. This has an impact on the organisms that can survive in the stream.

Organisms that can cope with pollution include the rat-tailed maggot, the bloodworm, the water louse and the sludge worm. However, some organisms are very sensitive to this type of water pollution so they are not found in areas where the levels are high.

Organisms such as mayfly and stonefly larvae are killed by high levels of water pollution (they cannot tolerate low oxygen levels), so they are indicators of clean water.

Air quality can be measured using lichens as **indicator species**.

Lichens →

Few lichens indicate high concentration of sulfur dioxide in the air

Lichens

Many lichens indicate low concentration of sulfur dioxide in the air

Rat-tailed maggot

Stonefly nymph

Predator–prey relationships

Animals that kill and eat other animals are called **predators** (e.g. foxes, lynx). The animals that are eaten are called **prey** (e.g. rabbits, snowshoe hares).

Many animals can be both predator and prey. For instance, a stoat is a predator when it hunts rabbits and it is the prey when it is hunted by a fox.

To demonstrate predator/prey cycles, do the following.
➤ Cut out multiple pictures of the animals in a particular predator–prey relationship (e.g. foxes and rabbits).
➤ Show these animals grouped together – try 5 foxes and 15 rabbits.
➤ Add 3 foxes. How will this affect the number of rabbits?
➤ Explain this to a revision buddy.
➤ Now show the changes in number of both rabbits and foxes as time goes by. Ask your buddy to rate your explanation.
➤ Swap roles.

Predator – stoat

Predator – fox

Prey – rabbit

Prey – stoat

In nature there is a delicate balance between the population of a predator (e.g. lynx) and its prey (e.g. snowshoe hare). However, the prey will always outnumber the predators.

The number of predators and prey follow a classic population cycle. There will always be more hares than lynx and the population peak for the lynx will always come after the population peak for the hare. As the population cycle is cause and effect, they will always be out of phase.

Normal prey population (they outnumber predators)

Predator population increases as plenty of food is available

Decrease in prey population as more are being eaten by increased number of predators

Decrease in predator population as there is now not enough food

39

1. What would the presence of stonefly nymphs tell you about the quality of water in a river?

Materials within ecosystems are constantly being recycled and used to provide the substances that make up future organisms. Two of these substances are water and carbon.

Recycling

The water cycle

Water is a vital part of the **biosphere**. Most organisms consist of over 50% water.

The two key processes that drive the water cycle are **evaporation** and **condensation**.

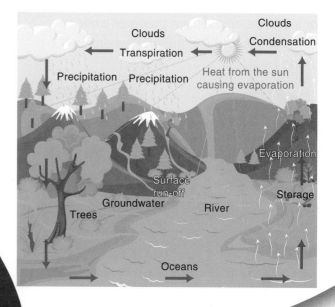

The carbon cycle

The constant recycling of carbon is called the carbon cycle.

➤ Carbon dioxide is removed from the atmosphere by green plants for photosynthesis.

➤ Plants and animals respire, releasing carbon dioxide into the atmosphere.

➤ Animals eat plants and other animals, which incorporates carbon into their bodies. In this way, carbon is passed along food chains and webs.

➤ Microorganisms such as fungi and bacteria feed on dead plants and animals, causing them to decay. The microorganisms respire and release carbon dioxide gas into the air. Mineral ions are returned to the soil through decay.

➤ Some organisms' bodies are turned into fossil fuels over millions of years, trapping the carbon as coal, peat, oil and gas.

➤ When fossil fuels are burned (combustion), the carbon dioxide is returned to the atmosphere.

Controlling decomposition

Intensive use of the land removes naturally occurring nitrates, phosphates and other essential mineral nutrients for plants. Farmers can restore these nutrients by applying inorganic fertiliser or using **organic** means, e.g. **compost** or manure. Farmers and gardeners produce compost for the soil from waste plant material.

Making compost

In order for decay microorganisms to carry out decomposition, they require:

➤ oxygen (as the process is aerobic)
➤ moisture
➤ a warm temperature.

The presence of any of these factors will increase the rate of decomposition.

One of your required practicals will be to investigate the effect of one factor on the rate of decay.

Keywords

Biosphere ➤ Area on the Earth's crust that is inhabited by living things
Organic ➤ Material obtained from living things; either their dead bodies or their waste. Organic can also refer to a type of farming that avoids overuse of intensive practices such as pesticides and inorganic fertilisers
Compost ➤ Fertiliser produced from the decay of organic plant material

Biogas digesters

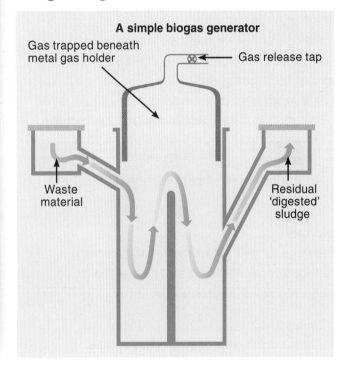

A simple biogas generator

Gas trapped beneath metal gas holder

Gas release tap

Waste material

Residual 'digested' sludge

Anaerobic decay produces methane gas (sometimes called **biogas**). Biogas can be made on a large scale using a continuous-flow method in a digester. Organic material is added daily and the biogas is siphoned off and stored. The remaining solid sludge can be used as fertiliser for crops.

The biogas produced by the digesters can be:
➤ burned to generate electricity
➤ burned to produce hot water and steam central heating systems
➤ used as a fuel for buses.

Construct a collage or model that displays the features of an organic small-holding farm. It should include annotations/descriptions of:
➤ compost heaps
➤ biodigesters
➤ biogas-driven electricity generators
➤ sludge tanks for storage of animals' waste.

1. Which two processes drive the water cycle?
2. How can carbon be stored in rocks?
3. Name two processes that add carbon dioxide to the atmosphere.
4. List three conditions needed for the successful decay of organic material.
5. Which combustible chemical is found in biogas?

Environmental change & biodiversity

Environmental change

Waste management

The human population is increasing exponentially (i.e. at a rapidly increasing rate). This is because birth rates exceed death rates by a large margin.

So the use of finite resources like fossil fuels and minerals is accelerating. In addition, waste production is going up:

➤ **on land**, from domestic waste in landfill, toxic chemical waste, **pesticides** and **herbicides**
➤ **in water**, from sewage fertiliser and toxic chemicals
➤ **in the air**, from smoke, carbon dioxide and sulfur dioxide.

Acid rain

When coal or oils are burned, sulfur dioxide is produced. Sulfur dioxide and nitrogen dioxide dissolve in water to produce acid rain.

Acid rain can:

➤ damage trees, stonework and metals
➤ make rivers and lakes acidic, which means some organisms can no longer survive.

The acids can be carried a long way away from the factories where they are produced. Acid rain falling in one country could be the result of fossil fuels being burned in another country.

The greenhouse effect and global warming

The diagram explains how global warming can lead to climate change. This in turn leads to lower biodiversity.

Small amount of infrared radiation transmitted to space

CO_2 and CH_4 in the atmosphere absorb some of the energy and radiate it back to Earth

Rays from the Sun reach Earth and are reflected back towards the atmosphere

The consequences of global warming are:

➤ a rise in sea levels leading to flooding in low-lying areas and loss of habitat

➤ the migration of species and changes in their distribution due to more extreme temperature and rainfall patterns; some organisms won't survive being displaced into new habitats, or newly migrated species may outcompete native species. The overall effect is a loss of biodiversity.

WS You may be asked to evaluate methods used to address problems caused by human impact on the environment.

For example, here are some figures relating to quotas and numbers of haddock in the North Sea in two successive years.

	2009	2010
Haddock quota (tonnes)	27 507	23 381
Estimated population (thousands)	102	101

What conclusions could you draw from this data? What additional information would you need to give a more accurate picture?

Create a board game called 'Conservation' that has 100 squares. The object of the game is to improve the quality and quantity of the world's ecosystems. The winner is the first person to reach square 100.

Here is an idea for a **bonus** square.
➤ Establish a breeding programme for endangered snow-leopards. (Throw the dice again.)

Here is an idea for a penalty square.
➤ Deforestation of Brazilian rainforest lowers biodiversity. (Go back three spaces.)

Try to grade bonuses and penalties according to their impact.

Keywords

Pesticide ➤ Chemical sprayed on crops to kill invertebrate pests
Herbicide ➤ Chemical sprayed on crops to kill weeds
Carbon sinks ➤ Resources that lock up carbon in their structure rather than allowing them to form carbon dioxide, e.g. peat bogs, oceans, limestone deposits
Endangered ➤ Category of risk attached to rare species of plants and animals. This usually triggers efforts to preserve the species' numbers
Emissions ➤ Gaseous products usually connected with pollution, e.g. carbon dioxide emissions from exhausts
Regeneration ➤ Rebuilding or regrowth of a habitat, e.g. flooding peatland to encourage regrowth of mosses and other plants

Biodiversity

Biodiversity is a measure of the number and variety of species within an ecosystem. A healthy ecosystem:

➤ has a large biodiversity
➤ has a large degree of interdependence between species
➤ is stable.

Species depend on each other for food, shelter and keeping the external physical environment maintained. Humans have had a negative impact on biodiversity due to:

➤ pollution killing plants and animals
➤ degrading the environment through deforestation and removing resources such as minerals and fossil fuels
➤ over-exploiting habitats and organisms.

Only recently have humans made efforts to reduce their impact on the environment. It is recognised that maintaining biodiversity is important to ensure the continued survival of the human race.

Impact of land use

As humans increase their economic activity, they use land that would otherwise be inhabited by living organisms. Examples of habitat destruction include:

A marble quarry

➤ farming
➤ quarrying
➤ dumping waste in landfill.

Peat bogs

Peat bogs are important habitats. They support a wide variety of organisms and act as **carbon sinks**.

If peat is burned it releases carbon dioxide into the atmosphere and contributes to global warming. Removing peat for use as compost in gardens takes away the habitat for specialised animals and plants that aren't found in other habitats.

Peat cut and left to dry

Deforestation

Deforestation is a particular problem in tropical regions. Tropical rainforests are removed to:

➤ **release land for cattle and rice fields** – these are needed to feed the world's growing population and for increasingly Western-style diets
➤ **grow crops for biofuel** – the crops are converted to **ethanol-based** fuels for use in petrol and diesel engines. Some specialised engines can run off pure ethanol.

The consequences of deforestation are:

➤ There are fewer plants, particularly trees, to absorb carbon dioxide. This leads to increased carbon dioxide in the atmosphere and accelerated global warming.
➤ Combustion and decay of the wood from deforestation releases more carbon dioxide into the atmosphere.
➤ There is reduced biodiversity as animals lose their habitats and food sources.

Maintaining biodiversity

To prevent further losses in biodiversity and to improve the balance of ecosystems, scientists, the government and environmental organisations can take action.

➤ Scientists establish **breeding programmes** for **endangered species**. These may be captive methods where animals are enclosed, or protection schemes that allow rare species to breed without being poached or killed illegally.
➤ The government sets **limits** on **deforestation** and **greenhouse gas emissions**.

Environmental organisations:

➤ **protect and regenerate** shrinking habitats such as mangrove swamps, heathlands and coral reefs
➤ **conserve and replant** hedgerows around the margins of fields used for crop growth
➤ introduce and encourage **recycling** initiatives that reduce the volume of landfill.

1. Name one pollutant gas that contributes to acid rain.
2. The human population is increasing exponentially – what does this term mean?
3. Why is high biodiversity seen as a good thing?
4. What steps could you take to maintain the biodiversity of a British mixed woodland?

41

Energy and biomass in ecosystems

Trophic levels

Communities of organisms are organised in an ecosystem according to their feeding habits.

Food chains show:
- the organisms that consume other organisms
- the transfer of **energy** and **materials** from organism to organism.

Energy from the Sun enters most food chains when green plants absorb sunlight to **photosynthesise**. Photosynthetic and chemosynthetic organisms are the producers of **biomass** for the Earth. Feeding passes this energy and biomass from one organism to the next along the food chain.

A food chain

Green plant:
producer

Rabbit:
primary consumer

Stoat:
secondary consumer

Fox:
tertiary consumer

The arrow shows the flow of energy and biomass along the food chain.
- All food chains start with a **producer**.
- The rabbit is a herbivore (plant eater), also known as the **primary consumer**.
- The stoat is a carnivore (meat eater), also known as the **secondary consumer**.
- The fox is the top carnivore in this food chain, the **tertiary consumer**.

Each consumer or producer occupies a **trophic level** (feeding level).
- Level 1 are producers.
- Level 2 are primary consumers.
- Level 3 are secondary consumers.
- Level 4 are tertiary consumers.

Excretory products and uneaten parts of organisms can be the starting points for other food chains, especially those involving **decomposers**.

Decomposers

Pyramids of biomass

Pyramids of biomass deal with the dry mass of living material in the chain. The width of each trophic level can be calculated by multiplying the number of organisms by their dry mass.

Hawk
Thrushes
Slugs
Lettuces

Efficiency of energy transfer

If you know how much energy is stored in the living organisms at each level of a food chain, the efficiency of energy transfer can be calculated.

To do this, divide the amount of energy used usefully (e.g. for growth) by the total amount of energy taken in.

$$\text{energy efficiency (\%)} = \frac{\text{energy used usefully}}{\text{total energy taken in}} \times 100$$

Example: A sheep eats 100 kJ of energy in the form of grass but only 9 kJ becomes new body tissue; the rest is lost as faeces, urine or heat. Calculate the efficiency of energy transfer in the sheep.

$$\text{energy efficiency} = \frac{9}{100} \times 100$$
$$= 9\%$$

Similar efficiency calculations can be performed for biomass.

 During your course you will be expected to use formulae to answer questions and to re-arrange the subject of an equation. Calculating energy efficiency is one example of when you may need to do this.

For example, you might be given the energy efficiency for a particular trophic level and asked to find out the total energy taken in. In this case:

$$\text{energy efficiency (\%)} = \frac{\text{energy used usefully}}{\text{total energy taken in}} \times 100$$

would be re-arranged to form:

$$\text{total energy taken in} = \frac{\text{energy used usefully}}{\text{energy efficiency}} \times 100$$

Energy

The fox gets the last tiny bit of energy left after all the others have had a share. This explains why food chains rarely have fourth degree or fifth degree consumers – they would not get enough energy to survive.

The stoats run around, mate, excrete, keep warm, etc. They pass on about a tenth of all the energy they get from the rabbits.

The rabbits run around, mate, excrete, keep warm, etc. They pass on about a tenth of all the energy they get from the grass.

The Sun is the energy source for all organisms. However, only about 10% of the Sun's energy is captured in photosynthesis.

Biomass

The fox gets the remaining biomass.

The stoats lose quite a lot of biomass in faeces (egestion), urine (excretion), carbon dioxide and water (respiration).

The rabbits lose quite a lot of biomass in faeces (egestion), urine (excretion), carbon dioxide and water (respiration).

A lot of the biomass remains in the ground as the root system.

Keyword

Decomposers ➤ Microorganisms that break down dead plant and animal material by secreting enzymes into the environment. Small, soluble molecules can then be absorbed back into the microorganism by the process of diffusion

1. What is meant by a trophic level?
2. Why do the trophic levels in a pyramid of biomass decrease in size as you move towards the top carnivore?
3. List three ways in which energy is lost in a food chain.

Keywords

Yield ➤ The weight of living material harvested in farming and fishing

Eutrophication ➤ A process where nitrates and phosphates enrich waterways, causing massive growth of algae and loss of oxygen

Sustainability ➤ Carrying out human activity, e.g. farming, fishing and extraction of resources from the ground, so that damage to the environment is minimised or removed

Farming techniques

Intensive farming is characterised by:
➤ high **yields**
➤ use of mechanised planting and harvesting
➤ extensive use of inorganic fertilisers, pesticides and herbicides.

In order to maximise profits, food production efficiency is the priority. This is achieved by:
➤ restricting energy transfer from animals to the environment, e.g. keeping animals under cover
➤ limiting animals' movement
➤ controlling the temperature of the animals' surroundings.

For example, battery chickens and calves are placed in cages or pens. Fish can be grown in cages and fed high-protein diets.

Many people object to these practices because they think animal welfare has not been given a high enough priority.

Eutrophication

Overusing fertilisers in intensive farming can lead to **eutrophication**.

❶ Fertilisers or sewage can run into the water and pollute it. As a result, there are a lot of nitrates and phosphates, which leads to rapid growth of algae.

Algae

❷ The algal blooms reproduce quickly, then die and rot. They also block off sunlight, which causes underwater plants to die and rot.

Rotting plants

❸ The number of aerobic bacteria increase. As they feed on the dead organisms they use up oxygen. This causes larger organisms and plants to die because they are unable to respire.

Carry out a role-play exercise that mimics a debate between two opposing groups, such as intensive farming versus organic farming or conservationists versus the fishing industry.
➤ Ideally, this activity works best with at least four people (two people representing each group).
➤ Draw up the points you want to make. Include the science you have learned in this topic.
➤ Allow each side to make their case. Then ask an independent 'judge' to make a ruling.
➤ Evaluate the exercise – ask the judge what factors led them to make their decision.

Food security

Food security is a global issue. It recognises the importance of allowing the world's growing population to have access to an adequate diet. Greater industrialisation and higher standards of living are leading to changing diets in countries such as China. So-called 'Western diets' have a higher red meat content. This increases the demand for more land devoted to raising livestock.

Sustainable methods of food production are constantly sought, but many factors need to be taken into account when trying to achieve food security.

➤ Many developed countries have a demand for scarce food resources, meaning that some foods are transported many thousands of miles from their point of origin.

➤ Due to the massive use of pesticides, new pests develop that are resistant to existing chemicals. Pathogenic microorganisms also evolve to become resistant to methods of control such as antibiotics.

➤ Climate change means that some countries are deprived of rainfall, resulting in a failure of harvests. This leads to widespread famine and armed conflicts as populations migrate to find work and food.

➤ Cost of farming methods continues to rise.

In the future, agricultural solutions to the increasing problem of food security might include:

➤ the increased use of hydroponics – a way of growing plants without soil under very controlled conditions

➤ biological control – where natural invertebrate predators are used to control pests

➤ gene technology – including pest-resistant GM crops

➤ fertilisers and pesticides.

Sustainable fishing

Fish stocks are declining across the globe. The problem is so big that unless methods are used to halt the decline, some species (such as the northwest Atlantic cod) might disappear.

Methods to make fishing sustainable include:

➤ governments imposing **quotas** that limit the weight of fish that can be taken from the oceans on a yearly basis – this practice is not always followed and illegal fishing is difficult to combat

➤ increasing the mesh size of nets to allow smaller fish to escape and reach adulthood, so that they can breed.

Biotechnology

Biotechnology, particularly the use of genetic engineering, has allowed new food substances to be produced relatively cheaply. Microorganisms can be grown in large industrial vats.

For instance, the fungus, Fusarium, can be used to produce **mycoprotein**, which is protein-rich and suitable for vegetarians. The fungus is grown on glucose syrup in **aerobic conditions** in a matter of days. Once grown, the biomass is **harvested** and **purified**.

GM crops can increase yields and add nutritional value by increasing the vitamin content of crops such as golden rice.

1. What factors threaten food security globally?
2. What are the advantages and disadvantages of keeping battery hens for food production?
3. Describe how biotechnology has improved food security in modern society.

Mind map

Quadrats

Transects

Pooters

Pitfall traps

Sweepnets

Capture/ recapture

Biotic factors

Keys

Intensive farming

Sustainable fishing

Farming techniques

Biotechnology

Farming and food security

Food security

Eutrophication

Trophic levels

Energy and biomass in ecosystems

Efficiency of energy transfer

Pyramids of biomass

Interdependence

Organisms and ecosystems

Communities

Adaptations

Taking measurements

Abiotic factors

Indicator species

Studying ecosystems

Quarrying

Landfill

Impact of land use

Deforestation

Biodiversity

Peat bogs

Predator–prey relationships

Maintaining biodiversity

Waste management

Global warming

ECOSYSTEMS

Environmental change

Greenhouse effect

Acid rain

The carbon cycle

Recycling

Biogas digesters

The water cycle

Controlling decomposition

Practice questions

1. Carbon is recycled in the environment in a process called the **carbon cycle**. The main processes of the carbon cycle are shown on the right.

    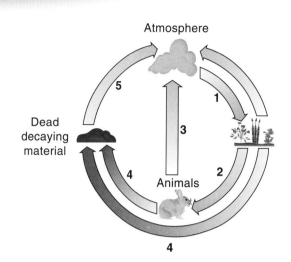

    a) Name the process that occurs at stage **3** in the diagram. **(1 mark)**

    b) The UK government is planning to use fewer fossil-fuel-burning power stations in the future. How might this affect the carbon cycle? Use ideas about **combustion** and **fossil fuel formation** in your answer. **(2 marks)**

2. An environmental scientist observed and measured a kingfisher and fish population in a county's rivers over 10 years. She recorded her results as a graph.

    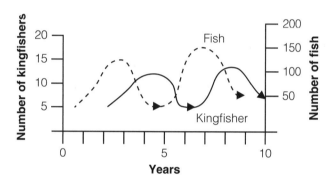

    a) How many fish were recorded in the third year? **(1 mark)**

    b) Describe how the size of the kingfisher population affected the size of the fish population. **(1 mark)**

    HT c) The scientist took her measurements by ringing and observing kingfishers on three rivers in the county. Fish numbers were estimated by counting the different species that anglers landed along the banks of the three rivers. Describe the limitations of these methods and suggest two ways in which the methods could be improved. **(6 marks)**

3. Choose the correct words to complete the following passage about adaptations. **(3 marks)**

    | environment | population | features | community |
    | characteristics | survival | evolutionary | predatory | suited |

    Adaptations are special .... or .... that make a living organism particularly well .... to its ....

    Adaptations are part of an .... process that increases a living organism's chance of ....

Answers

Page 5

1. **Prokaryotes:** any three bacteria or archaebacteria, e.g. cholera, *E. coli* and salmonella. **Eukaryotes:** any three from the plant, animal, protist or fungal kingdoms, e.g. geranium (plant), tiger (animal), amoeba (protist) and mushroom (fungus).
2. A prokaryote has a DNA loop and plasmids. A eukaryote's DNA is found in the nucleus.
3. True – all cells do have a cell membrane.
4. Mitochondrion.
5. Chloroplasts contain chlorophyll to absorb sunlight for photosynthesis.

Page 7

1. An organ.
2. It is able to contract (shorten).
3. Phloem.
4. **Any one benefit**, e.g. can be used to treat serious conditions, cancer research, organ transplants. Any one objection, e.g. the embryo has the potential to be a living human and shouldn't be experimented with, risk of viral transmission.

Page 9

1. **Any two from:** electron microscopes use electrons to form images, light microscopes use light waves; electron microscopes produce 2D and 3D images, light microscopes use 2D images only; electron microscopes have a magnification up to ×500 000 (2D), light microscopes have a magnification of up to ×1500; electron microscopes are able to observe small organelles, light microscopes are only able to observe cells and larger organelles; electron microscopes enable you to see things at high resolution, light microscopes allow you to see things at low resolution.
2. Food/nutrients, warmth and moisture/water.

Page 11

1. For growth, repair and reproduction.
2. Chromosomes.
3. **Mitosis:** asexual reproduction, repair and growth; **meiosis:** sexual reproduction.
4. DNA/chromosomes and all other organelles.

Page 13

1. **Building** – any one from: converting glucose to starch in plants/glucose to glycogen in animals; synthesis of lipid molecules, formation of amino acids in plants (which are built up into proteins). **Breaking down** – any one from: breaking down excess proteins to form urea, respiration.
2. Aerobic.
3. **Any two from:** transmitting nerve impulses, active transport, muscle contraction/movement, maintaining a constant body temperature, synthesis of molecules.
4. **Humans:** lactic acid; **yeast:** ethanol and carbon dioxide.

5. To pay back the oxygen debt, i.e. take in oxygen to remove the lactic acid in muscles.

Page 15

1. pH and temperature.
2. A substrate molecule fits exactly into a specific enzyme's active site.
3. It emulsifies fat and helps neutralise acid from the stomach.
4. Amino acids.

Page 17

1. **A:** cell membrane, **B:** DNA, **C:** cell wall, **D:** plasmid. (**1 mark for each correct**)
2. a) Lactic acid increase in muscles causes muscle fatigue/tiredness (**1 mark**); lactic acid is toxic (**1 mark**).
   b) Anaerobic respiration releases lower amounts of energy than aerobic respiration; not enough energy available for extended periods of intense activity. (**1 mark**)
   c) Glucose is completely broken down (to carbon dioxide and water). (**1 mark**)
3. a) Denaturing/denaturation. (**1 mark**)
   b) Change in shape of active site (**1 mark**); substrate no longer fits active site (**1 mark**).
4. Answer is 82.61 mm² (**2 marks**)
   Mean radius = 5.13 mm (**1 mark**); cross-sectional area = 3.14 × (5.13)² = 82.61 mm (**1 mark**)

Page 19

1. A shrew – the proportion of its area to its volume is greater, despite the fact that its **total** body area is less than that of an elephant.
2. The plant cells have a higher water potential/lower solute concentration. The water moves **down** an osmotic gradient from inside the cells into the salt solution.

Page 21

1. Root hair cells.
2. To allow space for gases to be exchanged more freely.
3. So that cells can freely carry water up the plant.

Page 23

1. It would increase the (evapo)transpiration rate.
2. When temperatures are high (during the day) and loss of water through open stomata would cause the plant to dehydrate and wilt.
3. Osmosis.
4. Water enters the xylem at root level due to a 'suction' force caused by evaporation from the leaves, called (evapo) transpiration. The water is drawn up as a column within the stem's xylem.

Page 25

1. Valves prevent backflow of blood and ensure it reaches the heart (especially from parts of the body vertically below the heart).
2. Excess fat (particularly saturated fat) in the diet causes cholesterol to build up and block the coronary artery. This restricts the

supply of blood to the heart muscle, which then does not receive enough oxygen and glucose. The heart muscle therefore dies.

Page 27

1. **Red blood cells** do not have a nucleus, are biconcave in shape, contain haemoglobin and carry oxygen. **Lymphocytes** have a nucleus, are irregular in shape and are involved in the immune response.
2. Oxygen is breathed into alveoli, diffuses across alveolar wall and combines with haemoglobin in a red blood cell. Blood enters the heart, from which it is pumped to the respiring muscle tissue. The oxygen diffuses from the red blood cell into a muscle cell, where it reacts with glucose during aerobic respiration.

Page 29

1. Photosynthesis takes **in** carbon dioxide and water, and requires an energy input. It produces glucose and oxygen. Respiration **produces** carbon dioxide and water, and releases energy. It absorbs glucose and oxygen.
2. Balancing investment costs with increased profit from increased yield.

Page 31

1. **a**, **d** and **e** (**1 mark** for each correct answer)
2. a) Healthy man (**1 mark**)
   b) **Any two from:** less oxygen absorbed into blood; longer diffusion distance across alveolar wall; insufficient oxygen delivered to muscles to release energy for exercise (**2 marks**)
3. a) **A:** artery (**1 mark**); **B:** vein (**1 mark**).
   b) **Any one from:** an artery has to withstand/recoil with higher pressure; elasticity allows smoother blood flow/second boost to blood when recoils. (**1 mark**)
   c) **Any one from:** to prevent backflow of blood; compensate for low blood pressure. (**1 mark**)

Page 33

1. **Any three from:** smoking tobacco, drinking excess alcohol, carcinogens, ionising radiation.
2. The body is more prone to infections.

Page 35

1. Cholera bacteria are found in human faeces, which contaminate water supplies.
2. **Any two reasonable answers, e.g.:** measles, Ebola, athlete's foot.

Page 37

1. Phagocyte engulfs a pathogen where it is digested by the cell's enzymes.
2. Lymphocytes detect antigen; this triggers production of antibodies; once pathogens are destroyed, memory cells are produced; further infection with same pathogen dealt with swiftly, as antibodies produced rapidly in large numbers. The process can also be triggered via vaccination.

1. An antibiotic is a drug that kills bacteria; an antibody is a protein produced by the immune system that kills bacteria.
2. An antiviral alleviates symptoms of an infection; analgesics are painkillers.
3. Do not prescribe antibiotics for viral/non-serious infections; ensure that the full course of antibiotics is completed.

Page 41

1. Human volunteers; computer simulations/modelling; cells grown in tissue culture.
2. **Any two from:** cancer treatment, pregnancy testing kits, measuring hormone levels, research.

Page 43

1. **Any three from:** stunted growth, leaf spots, areas of decay, growths/tumours, malformed stems and leaves, discolouration, presence of pests.
2. Photosynthesis and growth is affected.

Page 45

1. Bacterium – cholera; fungus – athlete's foot; virus – HIV; protist – malaria.
   (**3 marks** for all answers correct; **2 marks** for 2 or 3 answers correct; **1 mark** for 1 answer correct)
2. a) i) Phagocytes engulf the pathogen, then digest it. **(1 mark)**
      ii) Antibodies lock onto antigen/pathogen/clump pathogens together. **(1 mark)**
   b) Vaccine contains dead/heat-treated pathogen/microbe. **(1 mark)** Antigen recognised as foreign **(1 mark)**; lymphocytes produce antibodies against it **(1 mark)**; memory cells remain in system ready to produce antibodies if re-infection occurs **(1 mark)**.
   c) Antibiotics don't work against viruses **(1 mark)**; over-prescription may lead to antibiotic resistance **(1 mark)**.
   d) **Any one from:** antiviral drug/analgesic **(1 mark)**
3. a) Yes (no marks). Any two for **2 marks**: DDD results in a greater weight loss; 5.8 compared with 3.2; significantly higher than the placebo.
      No (no marks). Any two for **2 marks**: Number of volunteers for the DDD trial is very small compared with the other two trials; more trials need to be carried out; data is unreliable.
   b) In a double blind trial, neither the volunteers nor the doctors know which drug has been given **(1 mark)**; this eliminates all bias from the test/scientists cannot influence the volunteers' response in any way **(1 mark)**.

Page 47

1. **Any two from:** osmoregulation/water balance; balancing blood sugar levels; maintaining a constant body temperature; controlling metabolic rate.
2. The pituitary.

Page 49

1. Axons/dendrites.
2. They ensure a rapid response to a threatening/harmful stimulus, e.g. picking up a hot plate. As a result, they reduce harm to the human body.
3. Flow diagram with the following labels: (stretch) receptor at knee joint stimulated; sensory neurone sends impulse to spine; intermediate/relay neurone relays impulse to motor neurone; motor neurone sends impulse to (thigh) muscle; (thigh) muscle contracts.

Page 51

1. The frontal lobe, which is part of the cerebral cortex.
2. A CT scan is an X-ray test producing cross-sectional images of the brain using computer programs. A PET scan shows how body tissues are working and what they look like. PET scanners work by detecting radiation given off by radiotracers.
3. Sweating increases, vasodilation, hairs lower.

Page 53

1. The iris.
2. More convex/fatter.
3. An eyeball that is too short/a lens that stays too long and thin.

Page 55

1. It releases a range of hormones that control other processes in the body.
2. In the ovaries and the pituitary (female); in the testes (male).
3. Reduced ability of cells to absorb insulin and therefore high levels of blood glucose. This leads to tiredness, frequent urination, poor circulation, eye problems, etc.

Page 57

1. **Any three from:** glucose, amino acids, fatty acids, glycerol, some water.
2. Makes urine more concentrated.
3. It diffuses down a concentration gradient from the patient's blood into the dialysis fluid.

Page 59

1. FSH acts on the ovaries, causing an egg to mature; oestrogen inhibits further production of FSH, stimulates the release of LH and promotes repair of the uterus wall; LH stimulates release of an egg; progesterone maintains the lining of the uterus after ovulation has occurred and inhibits FSH and LH.
2. Just after menstruation has stopped/from day 7.
3. **Any one from:** production of sperm in testes; development of muscles and penis; deepening of the voice; growth of pubic, facial and body hair.

Page 61

1. Oral contraceptive, hormone injection or implant.
2. They provide a barrier/prevent transferral of the virus during sexual intercourse.
3. Microscopes enable scientists to observe in vitro fertilisation and retrieval of zygote/fertilised egg for implantation in the woman.

Page 63

1. **Shoots:** the auxin promotes growth; **roots:** the auxin inhibits growth.
2. Auxin to kill weeds; gibberellins to promote fruit growth.
3. Gibberellins.

Page 65

1. a) Stimulus. **(1 mark)**
   b) The response is automatic/unconscious **(1 mark)**; response is rapid **(1 mark)**.
   c) Stimulus at receptor triggers sensory neurone to send impulse **(1 mark)**; impulse received in brain and/or spinal cord and signal sent to intermediate/relay neurone **(1 mark)**; impulse then sent to motor neurone **(1 mark)**; motor neurone sends impulse to effector/muscles in hand **(1 mark)**.
2. a) The person's blood sugar level **(1 mark)** fluctuates dramatically **(1 mark)**.
   b) The person has eaten their breakfast at A and their lunch at B. **(1 mark)**
   c) There would be a slight rise in blood sugar level, followed by a swift drop back to normal level. **(1 mark)**
   d) Their blood sugar level had dropped too low/below normal. **(1 mark)**
3. a) They release (more) sweat **(1 mark)**; sweat evaporates, taking heat from the skin **(1 mark)**.
   b) Excretion. **(1 mark)**
   c) Amino acids. **(1 mark)**
   d) **Top box:** Urea enters/is carried in blood **(1 mark)**; **box below it:** Urine stored in bladder **(1 mark)**.

Page 67

1. It allows variation, which gives an evolutionary advantage when the environment changes.
2. Via runners.
3. **Any one from:** produces clones of the parent – if these are successfully adapted individuals, then rapid colonisation and survival can be achieved; only one parent required; fewer resources required than sexual reproduction; faster than sexual reproduction.

Page 69

1. It has allowed the production of linkage maps that can be used for tracking inherited traits from generation to generation. This has led to targeted treatments for these conditions.
2. Proteins.

Page 71

1. mRNA is involved in transcription and carries the coding sequence from the nucleus to the ribosome. tRNA is in ribosomes and involved in the translation process, i.e. building polypeptides/proteins from individual amino acids.
2. Wrong base sequences may lead to incorrect or no protein being produced. This may have consequences for health/wrong base sequence may not affect function of protein produced.

Page 73

1. Zero/0%.
2. XX.
3. Causes production of thick mucus in respiratory pathways and interferes with enzyme production.

Page 75

1. **Any two from:** the fossil record; comparative anatomy (pentadactyl limb); looking at changes in species during modern times; studying embryos and their similarities; comparing genomes of different organisms.
2. The conditions for their formation are rare, e.g. rapid burial and a lower chance of being discovered before they are eroded.

Page 77

1. **Evolution:** the long-term changes seen in species over a long period of time. **Natural selection:** the mechanism by which evolution occurs.
2. **Any two examples,** e.g. Kettlewell's moths; antibiotic resistance in bacteria.
3. They must be passed on by the well-adapted individual that contains them, through reproduction, to the next generation.

Page 79

1. In Darwin's theory, change in the inherited material occurs first. This leads to change in the phenotype/external appearance. Lamarck's theory stated that the physical change occurs first.
2. Mendel showed that characteristics could be passed down as 'units' (genes) in a predictable way.
3. Cloning allows mass production of individuals with beneficial traits in a short space of time.

Page 81

1. Genetic engineering is more precise and it takes less time to see results.
2. **Reason for:** food production improved through increased yields and better nutritional content. **Reason against:** GM plants may spread their genetic material into the wider ecosystem, resulting in, for example, herbicide-resistant weeds/ possible harmful effect of GM foods on consumers.

Page 83

1. Genus and species.
2. Invertebrates, vertebrates, protists, higher plants.
3. Common ancestor.

Page 85

1. **Any four from:**
   - adapted to environment/had different characteristics
   - named examples of different characteristics, e.g. some horse-like mammals had more flipper-like limbs (as whales have flippers); idea of competition for limited resources
   - examples of different types of competition; idea of survival of the fittest

   - adaptations being advantageous to living in water/idea that adaptations helped them survive
   - named examples of different adaptations, e.g. some horse-like mammals had more flipper-like limbs that allowed them to swim well in water; idea of inheritance of successful characteristics
   - (named) characteristics/adaptations passed on (through breeding). **(4 marks)**
2. a) Ff
   b) ff
3. a) **Step 3:** section of human DNA inserted into plasmid by ligase enzyme **(1 mark)**. **Step 5:** bacterium replicates/cultivated in fermenter. **(1 mark)**
   b) Restriction enzyme. **(1 mark)**
4. a) Nitrogenous base. **(1 mark)**
   b) Double helix. **(1 mark)**

Page 87

1. A **habitat** is the part of the physical environment in which an animal lives. An **ecosystem** includes the habitat, its communities of animals and plants, together with the physical factors that influence them.
2. **A mixed-leaf woodland:** the biodiversity is greater and so the links between different organisms are more extensive.
3. A **population** is the number of individuals of a species in a defined area. A **community** contains many different populations of species.
4. **Any two examples**, e.g. chemotrophs (live in deep ocean trenches and volcanic vents) and icefish (exist in waters less than 0°C in temperature).
5. So that they survive to reproductive age and pass on their genes to the next generation.

Page 89

1. Where you have a transition from one habitat to the next. It would tell you how numbers of different species vary along the line of the transect.

Page 91

1. The water is relatively clean.

Page 93

1. Condensation and evaporation.
2. As coal.
3. **Any two from:** combustion, animal respiration, plant respiration, microbial respiration (including decay).
4. Moisture, warmth and oxygen.
5. Methane.

Page 95

1. **One from:** sulfur dioxide; nitrogen dioxide.
2. Numbers increase at a rapidly increasing rate.
3. With more species, there are more relationships between different organisms and therefore more resistance to disruption from outside influences.
4. Plant a variety of trees, especially deciduous; protect rare species; make it a Site of Special Scientific Interest (SSSI);

protect against invasive species, e.g. red squirrel.

Page 97

1. The level that an organism feeds at, e.g. producer, primary consumer level. It refers to layers in a pyramid of biomass.
2. Most energy is lost to the environment between one trophic level and the next.
3. **Any three from:** respiration; movement; reproduction; maintaining constant body temperature; urine; faeces; not all parts of the animal/plant are eaten.

Page 99

1. Over fishing; demand for rarer foods by developed countries; growing world population; climate change; pesticide resistance.
2. **Advantages:** cheap cost of production; rapid growth of stock. **Disadvantage:** reduced animal welfare.
3. New varieties of plants with greater yields have been produced. Production of mycoprotein uses microorganisms and does not require farming animals.

Page 101

1. a) Respiration. **(1 mark)**
   b) **Any two from:** Fossil fuels represent a carbon 'sink'/they absorbed great quantities of carbon many millions of years ago from the atmosphere; combustion in power stations returns this carbon dioxide; less burning of fossil fuels cuts down on carbon emissions; alternative sources of energy may not return as much carbon dioxide to the atmosphere. **(2 marks)**
2. a) 120–125 **(1 mark)**
   b) When kingfishers increase, fish decrease/when kingfishers decrease, fish increase. **(1 mark)**
   c) This is a model answer, which demonstrates quality written communication (QWC) and would score the full **6 marks:** Three rivers is too small a sample so not all birds would be observed, and ringing birds might affect their survival. Some fish may evade capture by anglers and not all anglers will cooperate with the scientist. Not all species will be caught and kingfishers do not feed on every species of fish. Improvements could be made by sampling many more rivers, using more observers, sampling fish directly, e.g. mark/ recapture technique, observing which species of fish the kingfishers take, or by using more efficient capture methods for fish, e.g. netting.
3. a) features; characteristics (either way around); suited; environment; evolutionary; survival. (**6 words correct = 3 marks, four or five words correct = 2 marks, two or three words correct = 1 mark, one or 0 words correct = 0 marks.**)

GCSE
Success

Biology

Exam Practice Workbook

Tom
Adams

Biology

Cell Biology

Transport Systems and Photosynthesis

Health, Disease and the Development of Medicines

Coordination and Control

Contents

Inheritance, Variation and Evolution

Ecosystems

Practice Exam Papers

Answers

1 This image shows some human liver cells, as seen through a very powerful light microscope.

(a) Which organelle is labelled X? .... (1)

(b) Unlike skin cells, these cells contain many mitochondria, but they cannot be seen in the image. Suggest why not. (1)

....

(c) Why do the cells have many mitochondria? (2)

....

....

(d) Liver cells have different features.
Arrange the features in order of size, starting with the largest. (2)

| gene | nucleus | cell | chromosome | cytoplasm |

....

2 **(a)** A student is observing bacterial cells under the high power lens of a light microscope. She cannot see a nucleus in the cells and concludes that the cells do not contain DNA. Explain why this conclusion is wrong. (1)

....

....

(b) Which of the following words best describes a bacterial cell? Tick (✓) **one** box. (1)

Prokaryotic ☐

Eukaryotic ☐

Multicellular ☐

Undifferentiated ☐

For more help on this topic, see Letts GCSE Biology Revision Guide pages 4–5

1 The diagram shows a fertilised egg cell (a zygote).

(a) The zygote is described as a **stem cell**. What does this term mean? (1)

....

(b) The zygote has a very different appearance to the root hair cell (pictured right). However, all cells have some structures in common. Write down **two** of these structures. (2)

1. ....

2. ....

2 **(a)** A student attends a school trip to a medical research laboratory, where he is given a talk from a scientist on the techniques and benefits of stem cell research.

Describe **two** applications of stem cell research that the scientist is likely to mention. (2)

1. ....

2. ....

(b) After the visit, one of the student's friends says she is opposed to stem cell research. Describe **one** objection that people have to stem cell research. (1)

....

....

3 A live sperm cell is observed under the microscope beating its tail. It moves across the field of view at a rate of 200 µm every 30 seconds.

Assuming the sperm travels at the same rate and in the same direction, how far will it have travelled in one hour? Give your answer in mm. (3)

....

For more help on this topic, see Letts GCSE Biology Revision Guide pages 6–7

Organisation and differentiation

Module 2

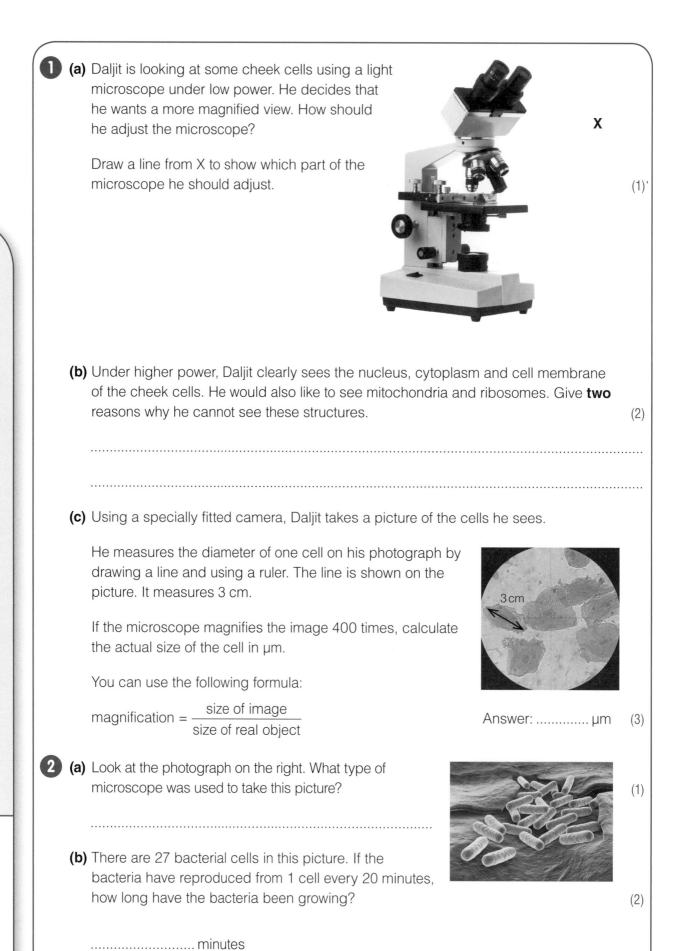

1 (a) Daljit is looking at some cheek cells using a light microscope under low power. He decides that he wants a more magnified view. How should he adjust the microscope?

Draw a line from X to show which part of the microscope he should adjust. (1)

X

(b) Under higher power, Daljit clearly sees the nucleus, cytoplasm and cell membrane of the cheek cells. He would also like to see mitochondria and ribosomes. Give **two** reasons why he cannot see these structures. (2)

....

....

(c) Using a specially fitted camera, Daljit takes a picture of the cells he sees.

He measures the diameter of one cell on his photograph by drawing a line and using a ruler. The line is shown on the picture. It measures 3 cm.

3 cm

If the microscope magnifies the image 400 times, calculate the actual size of the cell in μm.

You can use the following formula:

$$\text{magnification} = \frac{\text{size of image}}{\text{size of real object}}$$

Answer: .... μm   (3)

2 (a) Look at the photograph on the right. What type of microscope was used to take this picture? (1)

....

(b) There are 27 bacterial cells in this picture. If the bacteria have reproduced from 1 cell every 20 minutes, how long have the bacteria been growing? (2)

.... minutes

For more help on this topic, see Letts GCSE Biology Revision Guide pages 8–9

1 The illustrations show a single-celled organism, called an amoeba, and a multicellular organism (a horse).

Not to scale

Explain why the horse has specialised organs in its breathing and digestive system, and the amoeba has none. (2)

....

....

....

....

2 Complete the following table, which compares the processes of mitosis and meiosis. (3)

Mitosis	Meiosis
Involved in asexual reproduction	....
....	Produces variation
Produces cells with 46 chromosomes	....

3 Jenny is studying chicken cells and is looking at some examples down the microscope. She draws these cells.

(a) Which type of cell division is shown here? .... (1)

(b) Give a reason for your answer to **(a)**. (1)

....

4 Joshua wants to find out what happens to DNA molecules during cell division.

Complete the flow diagram to complete the sequence that DNA molecules go through when they replicate. (2)

Double helix 'unzips'	→	
		↓
	←	Enzyme bonds new bases together to form complementary strands

For more help on this topic, see Letts GCSE Biology Revision Guide pages 10–11

HT **1** Isaac is running a marathon. Write a balanced symbol equation for the main type of respiration that will be occurring in his muscles. (2)

....

2 Isaac's metabolic rate is monitored as part of his training schedule. He is rigged up to a metabolic rate meter. This measures the volumes of gas that he breathes in and out. The difference in these volumes represents oxygen consumption. This can be used in a calculation to show metabolic rate.

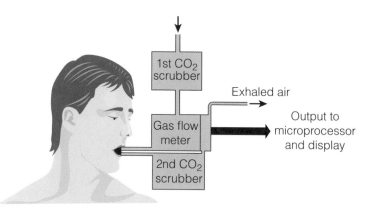

The table below shows some measurements taken from the meter over a period of one hour.

	Five minutes of jogging	Five minutes of rest	Five minutes of sprinting	Five minutes sprinting on an incline
Mean metabolic rate per ml oxygen used per kg per min	35	20	45	60

(a) The units of metabolic rate are expressed in the table as 'per kg'.
Why is this adjustment made? (2)

....

....

(b) Using the table, explain the difference in readings for jogging and sprinting. (2)

....

(c) Isaac does quite a lot of exercise. His friend Boris does not. How might Boris' readings compare with Isaac's? Give a reason for your answer. (2)

....

....

For more help on this topic, see Letts GCSE Biology Revision Guide pages 12–13

1 In an experiment to investigate the enzyme catalase, potato extract was added to a solution of hydrogen peroxide. The catalase in the potato catalysed the decomposition of the hydrogen peroxide and produced oxygen bubbles. The experiment was carried out at different temperatures and the results recorded in the table below.

Temperature / °C	0	10	20	30	40	50	60	70	80
Number of bubbles produced in one minute	0	10	24	40	48	38	8	0	0

(a) Plot a graph of these results on the graph paper. (3)

(b) Describe how the number of bubbles produced varies with the temperature of the reacting mixture. (2)

....

....

(c) Using the graph, estimate the optimum temperature for catalase to work at. (1)

....

(d) Factors other than temperature affect the activity of enzymes. Explain why the enzyme amylase, found in saliva, stops working when it gets to the stomach. (2)

....

....

For more help on this topic, see Letts GCSE Biology Revision Guide pages 14–15

1 Cells rely on diffusion as a way of transporting materials inwards and outwards.

(a) Name **two** substances that move by diffusion **into** animal cells. (2)

.... and ....

(b) Name **one** substance that might diffuse **out** of an animal cell. .... (1)

2 Osmosis is a special case of diffusion involving water. Plants rely on osmosis for movement of materials around their various structures.

On the right is a diagram of three plant cells in the root of a plant. Cell **A** has a higher concentration of water than cell **C**.

(a) Explain how water can keep moving from cell **A** to cell **C**. .... (3)

....

....

(b) Which of the following are examples of osmosis? Tick (✓) the **three** correct options. (3)

Water evaporating from leaves ☐

Water moving from plant cell to plant cell ☐

Mixing pure water and sugar solution ☐

A pear losing water in a concentrated solution of sugar ☐

Water moving from blood plasma to body cells ☐

Sugar being absorbed from the intestine into the blood ☐

3 Rabia is investigating how plant cells respond to being surrounded by different concentrations of sugar solution. She places some rhubarb tissue into pure water and then observes the cells under the microscope.

(a) Describe and explain the appearance of the rhubarb cells. (2)

....

....

(b) Rabia then puts some rhubarb tissue into a strong salt solution. Describe how the cells would change in appearance if she observed them under the microscope. (2)

....

....

For more help on this topic, see Letts GCSE Biology Revision Guide pages 18–19

1 This diagram shows a magnified view of the inside of a leaf. Complete the missing labels. (3)

Waxy cuticle

Palisade cells

Stoma

(a) ....

(b) ....

(c) ....

2 Plants all share a basic structure consisting of four main organs.

Describe the function that each organ performs in the plant. (4)

Roots: ....

Stem: ....

Leaf: ....

Flower: ....

3 Describe **three** adaptations of xylem vessels that make them suited to the job they do. (3)

....

....

4 The diagram shows xylem and phloem tissue.

(a) State **one** structural difference between the two tissues. (1)

....

....

Xylem Phloem

Xylem   Phloem

(b) Small, herbivorous insects called aphids are found on plant stems. They have piercing mouthparts that can penetrate down to the phloem.

Explain the reasons for this behaviour. (2)

....

....

For more help on this topic, see Letts GCSE Biology Revision Guide pages 20–21

Plant tissues, organs and systems

Module 8

1 In an experiment, a plant biologist carried out an investigation to measure the rate of transpiration in a privet shoot. She set up three tubes like the one in the diagram, measured their mass and exposed them each to different conditions.

- **A** – Left to stand in a rack

- **B** – Cold moving air from a fan was blown over it

- **C** – A radiant heater was placed next to it

The tubes were left for six hours and then their masses were re-measured. The biologist recorded the masses in this table.

Tube	A	B	C
Mass at start (g)	41	43	45
Mass after six hours (g)	39	35	37
Mass loss (g)	2	8	5
% mass loss	4.9		11.9

(a) Calculate the percentage mass loss in tube B. Show your working. (2)

....

....

(b) Which factor increased the rate of transpiration the most? .... (1)

(c) Evaporation from the leaves has increased in tubes B and C. Describe how this would affect water in the xylem vessels of the plant. (1)

....

2 Guard cells respond to light intensity by opening and closing stomata. Explain how this occurs. In your answer, use ideas about osmosis and turgidity. (6)

....

....

....

....

....

....

Continue your answer for this question on a separate piece of paper.

For more help on this topic, see Letts GCSE Biology Revision Guide pages 22–23

1 The graph shows the number of people who die from coronary heart disease per 100 000 people in different parts of the UK.

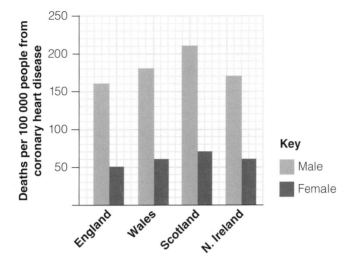

(a) (i) Which country has the highest number of deaths per 100 000? (1)

....

(ii) Calculate the difference between this country's death rate for males and the country with the smallest death rate for males. (1)

....

(b) Describe the pattern between death rates from coronary heart disease in men and women. (1)

....

2 The diagram shows the human circulatory system.

Match the numbers on the diagram with the words listed below. Write the appropriate numbers in the boxes. (4)

Artery ☐

Capillaries in the body ☐

Vein ☐

Capillaries in the lungs ☐

■ Deoxygenated blood   ■ Oxygenated blood

For more help on this topic, see Letts GCSE Biology Revision Guide pages 24–25

1. The table shows some data from an experiment measuring the effect of different doses of warfarin in two samples of rat blood. Warfarin prevents blood from clotting, killing the rat as a result of internal bleeding.

Warfarin dose / mg per kg body weight	Time for clot to form in sample 1	Time for clot to form in sample 2
0.2	52	61
0.4	101	99
0.6	193	197
0.8	300	311
1	978	984

(a) Calculate the average change in clotting rate between 0.2 and 1.0 mg of warfarin per kilogram of body weight. Show your working. (2)

....

....

(b) Explain why the warfarin dose was measured in mg per kg of body weight. (1)

....

(c) Describe the pattern of results shown in the data. (1)

....

2. Scientists are studying the performance of pearl divers living on a Japanese island. They have timed how long they can stay underwater. The scientists have also measured recovery time for the divers' breathing rates after a dive. The data is shown in the table below.

Vital capacity / litres	Max. time under water / mins
3.5	2.5
4.0	2.7
4.3	2.8
4.5	2.9
4.6	3.0

Vital capacity is the maximum volume of air that the lungs can hold at any one time.

One of the scientists suggests that having a larger vital capacity allows a diver to stay underwater for longer. Do you agree with her? Give a reason for your answer. (2)

Agree / disagree: ....

Reason: ....

....

For more help on this topic, see Letts GCSE Biology Revision Guide pages 26–27

HT **1** A student decided that he would test a green plant to see how the rate of photosynthesis changed with temperature. The graph shows the results he obtained.

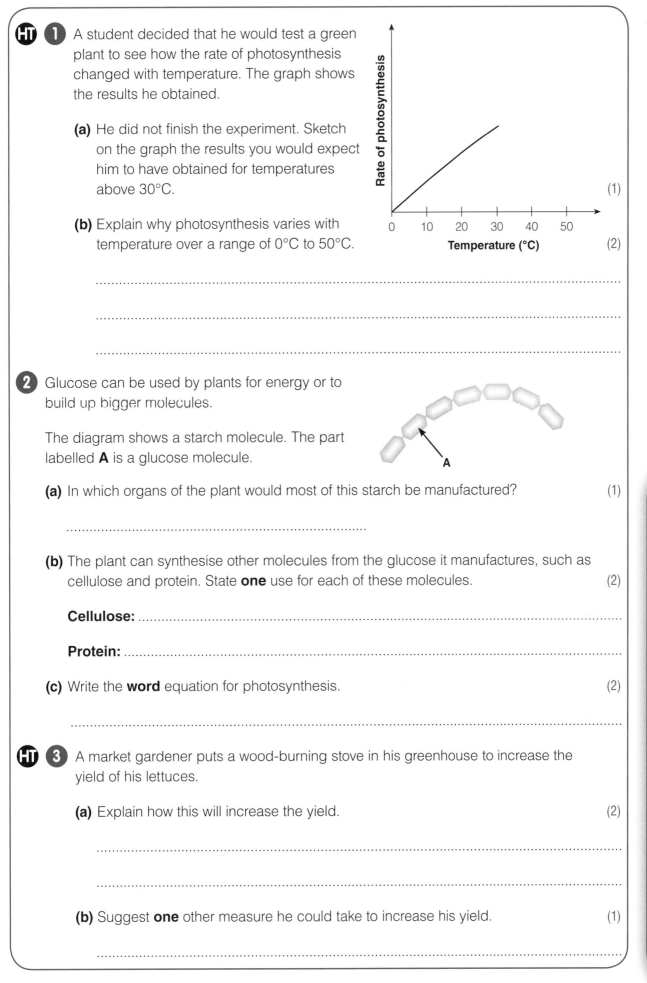

Rate of photosynthesis

0   10   20   30   40   50
Temperature (°C)

(a) He did not finish the experiment. Sketch on the graph the results you would expect him to have obtained for temperatures above 30°C. (1)

(b) Explain why photosynthesis varies with temperature over a range of 0°C to 50°C. (2)

....

....

....

2 Glucose can be used by plants for energy or to build up bigger molecules.

The diagram shows a starch molecule. The part labelled **A** is a glucose molecule.

A

(a) In which organs of the plant would most of this starch be manufactured? (1)

....

(b) The plant can synthesise other molecules from the glucose it manufactures, such as cellulose and protein. State **one** use for each of these molecules. (2)

Cellulose: ....

Protein: ....

(c) Write the **word** equation for photosynthesis. (2)

....

HT **3** A market gardener puts a wood-burning stove in his greenhouse to increase the yield of his lettuces.

(a) Explain how this will increase the yield. (2)

....

....

(b) Suggest **one** other measure he could take to increase his yield. (1)

....

For more help on this topic, see Letts GCSE Biology Revision Guide pages 28–29

Photosynthesis

Module 12

1 Obesity is a non-communicable condition. The table shows how obesity in a population of children aged between two and ten changed between 2005–2013.

Year	% of obese children
2005	9.9
2006	10.2
2007	10.8
2008	11.3
2009	11.8
2010	12.3
2011	12.8
2012	13.3
2013	13.7

(a) Predict the percentage of obese children in the UK for 2014 based on this trend. (1)

.............................%

(b) If the body's daily energy requirements are exceeded, sugar can be converted to storage products; for example, fat under the skin.
Name **one** other storage product and where it would be found. (2)

....

(c) Write down **two** other conditions / diseases that are non-communicable. (2)

....

....

2 The table shows how smoking can affect a person's chances of getting lung cancer.

Number of cigarettes smoked per day	Increased chance of lung cancer compared to non-smokers
5	×4
10	×8
15	×12
20	×16

(a) Estimate the increased chance of lung cancer if someone smoked 25 cigarettes a day. (1)

....

(b) Write down **one** harmful effect that smoking can have on unborn babies. (1)

....

....

For more help on this topic, see Letts GCSE Biology Revision Guide pages 32–33

1 Microorganisms consist of bacteria, viruses, fungi and protists. Many cause harm to the human body.

(a) Write down the term that describes these disease-causing organisms. (1)

....

(b) Harmful microorganisms produce symptoms when they reproduce in large numbers. Write down **two** ways in which microorganisms cause these symptoms. (2)

1. ....

2. ....

2 The picture below shows the bacterium that causes cholera.

(a) Write down **two** symptoms of cholera. (2)

1. ....

2. ....

(b) Explain why cholera spreads rapidly in natural disaster zones. (2)

1. ....

2. ....

3 Malaria kills many thousands of people every year. The disease is common in areas that have warm temperatures and stagnant water.

(a) Explain why this is. (2)

....

....

(b) A protist called *Plasmodium* lives in the salivary glands of the female *Anopheles* mosquito.

From the box below, choose a word that describes each organism. (2)

parasite	disease	symptom	vector	consumer	host

Mosquito: ....   **Plasmodium:** ....

(c) Samit, an African villager, believes that having mosquito nets around the beds of family members and taking antiviral remedies will reduce their risk of catching malaria.

Explain why he is only partially correct. (2)

....

....

Communicable diseases

Module 14

For more help on this topic, see Letts GCSE Biology Revision Guide pages 34–35

1 The diagram shows a white blood cell producing small proteins as part of the body's immune system.

(a) What is the name of these proteins?

.... (1)

(b) These proteins will eventually lock on to specific invading pathogens. Describe what happens next to disable the pathogens. (1)

....

....

(c) Below are the names of some defence mechanisms that the body uses. Match each defence mechanism with the correct function. The first one has been done for you. (3)

Epithelial cells in respiratory passages	engulf pathogens.
Phagocytes	contain enzymes called lysozymes that break down pathogen cells.
Tears	contains acid to break down pathogen cells.
Stomach	trap pathogens in mucus.

2 The graph shows the antibody levels in Dominic after he contracted the flu. The flu pathogen first entered his body two days before point X. There was then a second invasion at point Y.

(a) Name **one** transmission method by which Dominic could have caught the flu virus. (1)

....

(b) After how many days did the antibodies reach their maximum level? (1)

.... days

(c) What is the difference in antibody level between point Y and this maximum? Show your working. (2)

.... arbitrary units

(d) Explain, using your knowledge of memory cells, the difference between these two levels. (2)

....

....

For more help on this topic, see Letts GCSE Biology Revision Guide pages 36–37

1 The photograph shows the structure of the human immunodeficiency virus (HIV). For decades it has spread throughout the world, especially in developing countries.

A vaccine is now being developed that shows promising results. It works by mimicing the shapes and structures of HIV proteins. Scientists hope the immune system may be 'educated' to attack the real virus. A specially designed adenovirus shell can protect the vaccine genes until they are in a cell that can produce the vaccine protein.

Using your knowledge of the immune response and immunological memory, describe and explain how antibodies can be produced against the HIV virus. (6)

....

....

....

....

....

....

....

....

....

2 Explain why antibiotics are becoming increasingly less effective against 'superbugs' such as MRSA. (3)

....

....

....

....

For more help on this topic, see Letts GCSE Biology Revision Guide pages 38–39

Fighting disease

Module 16

1 A pharmaceutical company is carrying out a clinical trial on a new drug called alketronol. They are testing it to see whether it produces significant adverse (harmful) events in a sample of 226 patients.

(a) Apart from checking for adverse events, write down **two** other reasons that a company carries out clinical trials. (2)

1. ....

2. ....

(b) The kind of trial carried out is a double blind trial. What does this term mean? (2)

....

....

....

(c) Data from the trial is shown in the table below.

Adverse event	Alketronol	Placebo
	Number of patients	Number of patients
Pain	4	3
Cardiovascular	21	20
Dyspepsia	7	6
Rash	10	1

(i) Calculate the percentage of patients **in the trial** who suffered a cardiovascular event while taking alketronol. Show your working. (2)

.... %

(ii) A scientist is worried that alketronol may trigger heart attacks. Is there evidence in the data to support this view? Explain your answer. (2)

....

....

....

(iii) Which other adverse event might cause concern? Give a reason for your decision. (2)

....

....

For more help on this topic, see Letts GCSE Biology Revision Guide pages 40–41

1 Ash dieback, or *Chalara*, is caused by a fungus called *Hymenoscyphus fraxineus*. *Chalara* results in loss of leaves, crown dieback and bark damage in ash trees. Once a tree is infected, the disease is usually fatal because the tree is weakened and becomes prone to pests or pathogens.

The map gives an indication of where cases of *Chalara* were reported in 2012 in the UK.

Scientists have also discovered that:

- *Chalara* spores are unlikely to survive for more than a few days
- spores can be dispersed by winds blowing from mainland Europe
- trees need a high dose of spores to become infected
- there is a low probability of dispersal on clothing or animals and birds.

Key:
■ = infection confirmed

(a) Damage to leaves can be caused by lack of certain minerals that plants need.

Write down **one** mineral deficiency and how it can affect leaves.

Mineral deficiency: .... **Leaf appearance:** .... (2)

(b) Which **one** of the following conclusions is supported by evidence from the map?
Tick (✓) **one** box. (1)

Chalara is limited to the East of England. ☐

Spores of *Chalara* arrived in England by being carried on winds from Europe. ☐

There is a high concentration of *Chalara* cases in the East of England. ☐

Ash trees in north-west Scotland are resistant to *Chalara*. ☐

(c) One scientist suggests that cutting down and burning infected trees could eradicate the disease.

(i) Explain how this method could be effective. (2)

....

....

(ii) Give **one** reason why this control method may not stop the spread of *Chalara*. (1)

....

For more help on this topic, see Letts GCSE Biology Revision Guide pages 42–43

1 From the box below, choose three words to complete the information about how conditions are kept stable in the human body. (3)

effectors	spine	receptors	homeostasis	hormones	glands

Certain factors have to be kept constant in the body. This is achieved by a process called
.... In order for this to happen, the central nervous system (CNS) needs to receive information from the environment. This is accomplished through ....
such as light-sensitive cells on the retina. Once the information has been relayed, the CNS brings about appropriate changes through ....

HT **2** This diagram shows how production of the hormone adrenaline is controlled.

Hypothalamus → CRH Corticotropin-releasing hormone → Pituitary → ACTH Adrenocorticotropic hormone → Adrenal glands → Adrenaline

(a) What name is given to this process, where a system resists a change from a norm (set point) level? .... (1)

(b) Another hormone, cortisol, is produced by the adrenal glands. Its production is also governed by CRH and ACTH production, in the same way as adrenaline. Cortisol increases nutrient distribution, reduces inflammation, and also takes part in water control. In Addison's disease, the adrenal glands fail to produce enough cortisol.

(i) What is the effect of Addison's disease on the production of ACTH? (1)

....

(ii) Using the information above, give **one** symptom of Addison's disease. (1)

....

(iii) Here is some data taken from adult blood samples.

Patient	A	B	C	D	E
Cortisol in blood / µg per litre	31.0	19.2	20.5	1.2	16.0

Which patient is most likely to have Addison's disease? .... (1)

(iv) A doctor injects some cortisol into this patient's blood, then takes another sample. The reading is now 7 µg per litre. If we assume that the patient has 5 litres of blood in their body, calculate the amount of cortisol in this person's blood. Show your working. (2)

....

For more help on this topic, see Letts GCSE Biology Revision Guide pages 46–47

1 Complete the missing labels in this diagram of a motor neurone. (2)

(a) ....

Axon

Effector / muscle

(b) ....

2 A company is developing technology that allows robots to make decisions in a form of artificial intelligence. As part of their research, the company tries to model the human nervous system.

(a) Write down the name given to the part of the nervous system that processes information from the senses. .... (1)

(b) Describe the other parts of the human nervous system that would need to be reproduced so that the robots could detect stimuli in the environment. In your answer, use the words in the box below. (3)

| receptor | sensory neurone | brain |

....

....

....

3 The diagram shows a junction (**X**) between two nerve cells.

Impulse

X

Impulse

(a) What name is given to this nerve junction? .... (1)

(b) In order for the impulse to be transmitted from one neurone to the next, a transmitter substance needs to be released. Describe the sequence of events involved. (3)

....

....

....

For more help on this topic, see Letts GCSE Biology Revision Guide pages 48–49

1 The diagram shows the human brain.

X

(a) Write down the name of the part of the brain labelled X.

....

(1)

(b) Tick (✓) the **two** correct statements about the brain and its parts.

(2)

The cerebellum is responsible for controlling heartbeat. ☐

The brain contains junctions between all three types of neurone. ☐

The brain is part of the central nervous system. ☐

The medulla controls higher mental functions. ☐

2 Rafiq is enjoying a skiing holiday, but not the cold! His body is working hard to keep at a constant temperature.

(a) After standing while waiting for a ski lift, Rafiq starts to shiver. Explain how shivering helps him to maintain his temperature.

(2)

....

....

(b) After skiing cross-country for a while, Rafiq starts to sweat underneath his thermals. Explain how sweating enables him to lose heat.

(2)

....

....

(c) Rafiq's internal body temperature has changed very little during the day. What temperature is this likely to be? Circle the correct answer.

(1)

30°C	35°C	37°C	40°C	50°C

(d) Rafiq's blood vessels can undergo vasoconstriction. Explain how this helps him conserve heat.

(3)

....

....

....

For more help on this topic, see Letts GCSE Biology Revision Guide pages 50–51

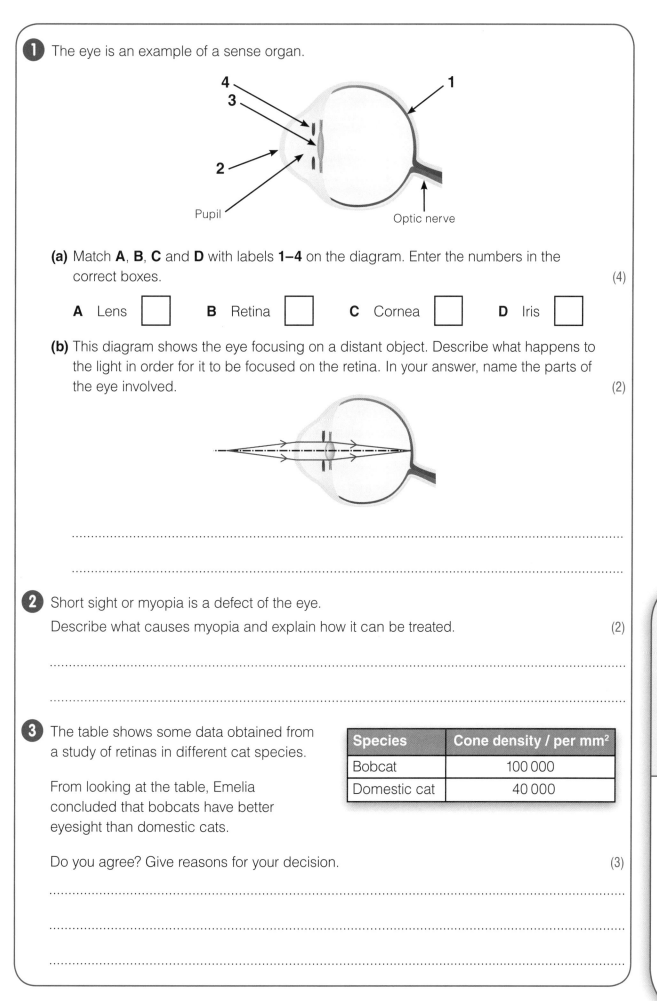

1 The eye is an example of a sense organ.

(a) Match **A**, **B**, **C** and **D** with labels **1–4** on the diagram. Enter the numbers in the correct boxes. (4)

A Lens ☐   **B** Retina ☐   **C** Cornea ☐   **D** Iris ☐

(b) This diagram shows the eye focusing on a distant object. Describe what happens to the light in order for it to be focused on the retina. In your answer, name the parts of the eye involved. (2)

....

....

2 Short sight or myopia is a defect of the eye.

Describe what causes myopia and explain how it can be treated. (2)

....

....

3 The table shows some data obtained from a study of retinas in different cat species.

From looking at the table, Emelia concluded that bobcats have better eyesight than domestic cats.

Do you agree? Give reasons for your decision. (3)

Species	Cone density / per mm²
Bobcat	100 000
Domestic cat	40 000

....

....

....

The eye

Module 22

For more help on this topic, see Letts GCSE Biology Revision Guide pages 52–53

1 Label the gland shown on the diagram and add the name of a hormone it produces. (2)

Gland:
Hormone:

2 A new nanotechnology device has been developed for people with diabetes – it can detect levels of glucose in the blood and communicate this information to a hormone implant elsewhere in the body. The implant releases a precise quantity of hormone into the bloodstream when required.

(a) Explain how this device could help a person with type 1 diabetes who has just eaten a meal. (2)

....

....

(b) Explain why a person with type 2 diabetes might not have as much use for this technology. (2)

....

....

3 Complete the missing information in the table, which is about different endocrine glands in the body. (4)

Gland	Hormones produced
Pituitary gland	.... and ....
Pancreas	Insulin and glucagon
....	Thyroxine
....	Adrenaline
Ovary	.... and ....
Testes	Testosterone

For more help on this topic, see Letts GCSE Biology Revision Guide pages 54–55

1 A marathon runner is resting the day before she competes in a race. The table shows the water that she gains and loses during the day.

Gained	Water gained (ml)	Lost	Water lost (ml)
In food	1000	In urine	
From respiration	300	In sweat	800
Drinking	1200	In faeces	100
Total gained		**Total lost**	2500

(a) How much water does the runner lose in urine during the day? .... (1)

(b) What can you say about the total water gained and the total water lost in the day? Why is this important? (2)

....

....

(c) The runner runs a marathon the next day. Suggest and explain how the figures shown in the table may alter during the day of the race. (4)

....

....

....

2 The diagram shows a nephron.

Your responses to the following questions should be **A**, **B** or **C**.

(a) Where does selective reabsorption occur? (1)

....

(b) Where does salt regulation occur? .... (1)

(c) In which region does filtration occur? .... (1)

(d) Explain how the brain and kidneys work together to restore water levels in the blood when the body is dehydrated. (4)

....

....

....

For more help on this topic, see Letts GCSE Biology Revision Guide pages 56–57

Water and nitrogen balance

Module 24

1 The graph shows the thickness of the uterus during the menstrual cycle. Use the graph and your scientific knowledge to explain what happens in the woman's ovaries and uterus between days 5 and 28. (3)

Day of cycle

....

....

....

2 Match each hormone with the correct description. The first one has been done for you. (3)

FSH	Oestrogen	Progesterone	LH

| promotes repair of the uterus wall **and** stimulates egg release. | maintains the lining of the uterus. | stimulates release of an egg **only**. | causes the egg to mature. |

HT 3 The diagram shows how the human process of ovulation is controlled.

(a) X represents an effect that two hormones have on the pituitary gland. Write down the name of this effect. .... (1)

(b) Name hormone Y. .... (1)

(c) Name hormone Z. .... (1)

(d) Describe the effect on hormone Z if the egg is fertilised. (2)

....

....

For more help on this topic, see Letts GCSE Biology Revision Guide pages 58–59

1 Tim and Margaret are finding it hard to conceive a child. They visit a fertility clinic and meet some other couples. The table shows some information about the problem that each couple has.

Couple	Problem causing infertility	Percentage of infertile couples with this problem	Percentage success rate of treatment
Tim and Margaret	Blocked fallopian tubes	13	20
Rohit and Saleema	Irregular ovulation	16	75
Leroy and Jane	No ovulation	7	95
Gary and Charlotte	Low sperm production	15	10
Ian and Kaye	No sperm production	21	10
Stuart and Mai	Unknown cause	28	–

(a) Which couple has the best chance of being successfully treated? (1)

....

(b) In how many of the six couples is the problem known to be with the female? (1)

....

(c) The treatment of irregular ovulation and no ovulation have the highest success rates. Explain why treating irregular ovulation would produce more pregnancies in the whole population. (2)

....

(d) Leroy and Jane are considering two methods to help them have children. The first is to have an egg donated by another woman. The second is to arrange for another woman to conceive the child using sperm from Leroy, then give birth to it (surrogacy). What are the advantages and disadvantages of each method? (4)

....

....

....

....

....

2 Explain how the contraceptive pill works. In your answer, name any hormones involved. (2)

....

....

....

For more help on this topic, see Letts GCSE Biology Revision Guide pages 60–61

Contraception and infertility

Module 26

1. Raj germinated a bean seed. Diagram **A** shows the bean after seven days. Raj then turned the bean onto its side (diagram **B**). Diagram **C** shows the bean a week later.

A   B   C

Explain fully why the plant responded in this way. (3)

....

....

....

2. Which substance does rooting powder contain that stimulates root growth?
Tick (✓) **one** box. (1)

Enzymes ☐   Nitrates ☐   Plant hormones ☐   Vitamins ☐

3. Miriam wants to find out if shoots will grow towards the light. Describe an experiment she could do to show this. Your answer should include:

• a method   • the likely results she would get. (6)

....

....

....

....

....

....

....

....

....

....

For more help on this topic, see Letts GCSE Biology Revision Guide pages 62–63

1 From the box below, choose **three** words to complete these sentences. (3)

| zygotes | gametes | diploid | haploid | mitosis | meiosis |

Eggs and sperm are .... They are .... because they contain one set of chromosomes. Eggs and sperm are produced in the ovaries and testes by ....

2 Tick (✓) the **two** statements about causes of variation that are true. (2)

Meiosis shuffles genes, which makes each gamete unique. ☐

Gametes fuse randomly. ☐

Zygotes fuse randomly. ☐

Mitosis shuffles genes, which makes each gamete the same. ☐

3

Sexual reproduction is the best strategy for organisms because it allows variation and therefore greater adaptation.

Asexual reproduction is better because when an organism is well adapted, it can produce exact copies of itself.

(a) John and Ayesha disagree about which type of reproduction is most beneficial to organisms. State which explanation, if any, is correct. Give the reasons for your choice. (3)

....

....

....

....

(b) Apart from variation, write down **one** other difference between sexual and asexual reproduction. (1)

....

....

(c) Describe how yeast carries out asexual reproduction. (2)

....

....

For more help on this topic, see Letts GCSE Biology Revision Guide pages 66–67

Sexual and asexual reproduction

Module 28

1 Tick (✓) the statements about the Human Genome Project (HGP) that are true. (3)

The genome of an organism is the entire genetic material present in its adult body cells. ☐

The data produced from the HGP produced a listing of amino acid sequences. ☐

The HGP involved collaboration between US and UK geneticists. ☐

The project allowed genetic abnormalities to be tracked between generations. ☐

The project was controversial as it relied on embryonic stem cells. ☐

2 Studies of genomes can help scientists work out the evolutionary history of organisms by comparing the similarity of particular DNA sequences that code for a specific protein.

The table shows the percentage DNA coding similarity for protein A in different organisms.

Species	% DNA coding similarity between species and humans for protein A
Human	100
Chimpanzee	100
Horse	88.5
Fish	78.6
Yeast	67.3
Protist	56.6

(a) What evidence is there in the table that closely related organisms developed from a recent common ancestor? (1)

....

(b) Using only the information from the table, which non-vertebrate is the most closely related to humans? .... (1)

3 The Human Genome Project has enabled specific genes to be identified that increase the risk of developing cancer in later life. Two of these genes are the *BRCA1* and *BRCA2* mutations that increase the risk of developing breast cancer.

(a) If women are prepared to take a genetic test, how could this information help doctors advise women about breast cancer? (2)

....

....

(b) If a woman possesses these mutations, it does not mean that she will definitely develop breast cancer. Why is this? (2)

....

....

For more help on this topic, see Letts GCSE Biology Revision Guide pages 68–69

1 The molecule DNA is a double helix made of two complementary strands.

(a) Write down the bases that pair with **T** and **C**. (1)

T pairs with ....

C pairs with ....

(b) How many bases code for **one** amino acid when a protein molecule is made? .... (1)

HT **2** Mutations occur when genes on DNA cause them to code for different proteins (or sequences of amino acids).

(a) State **two** causes of mutation. (2)

.... and ....

(b) A change occurs in a section of DNA that leads to a new protein being formed. Explain how this is possible and why the protein is not able to perform its function. (3)

....

....

....

HT **3** The diagram shows the processes that occur in the cell when a protein is coded for and produced. For each of the stages (1–4), describe and explain how the various molecules are involved. (4)

1   2   3   4   Not to scale

Nucleus   Ribosome   Amino acids

Stage 1:..

....

Stage 2:..

....

Stage 3:..

....

Stage 4:..

....

For more help on this topic, see Letts GCSE Biology Revision Guide pages 70–71

The genetic code

Module 30

1 Raj is the owner of two dogs, both of which are about two years old. Both dogs are black in colour and came from the same litter of puppies.

(a) A dog's adult body cell contains 78 chromosomes. How many chromosomes would be in a male dog's sperm cells? (1)

....

(b) The dogs' mother had white fur and the father had black fur. Using what you know about dominant genes, suggest why there were no white puppies in the litter. (2)

....

....

HT **(c)** One year later, one of the black puppies mated with a white-haired dog. She had four puppies. Two had black fur and two had white fur. The letters **B** and **b** represent the alleles for fur colour: **B** for black fur and **b** for white fur.

Draw a fully labelled genetic diagram to explain this. Show which offspring would be black and which would be white. (3)

2 Complete these two different crosses between a brown-eyed parent and a blue-eyed parent. (4)

(a)

	Brown eyes	×	Blue eyes
Parents	BB	×	bb

Gametes ○ ○ ○ ○

Offspring ○ ○ ○ ○

Phenotype □ □ □ □

(b)

	Brown eyes	×	Blue eyes
Parents	Bb	×	bb

Gametes ○ ○ ○ ○

Offspring ○ ○ ○ ○

Phenotype □ □ □ □

For more help on this topic, see Letts GCSE Biology Revision Guide pages 72–73

1 This is an evolutionary tree for some of our present-day vertebrates. Where possible, use the diagram to answer these questions.

Million years ago		Geological time period
	Snake Lizard	
50	Turtle Terrapin Tortoise Birds Crocodile	Tertiary
	Tuarta (giant lizard)	
		Cretaceous
100		
	Crocodilia	
	Dinosaurs	Jurassic
150		
		Triassic
200		Permian
	Testudina	
	Archosaurs	
250		
		Carboniferous
300	Sauropods	

(a) How many millions of years ago did the testudina appear? (1)

....

(b) (i) In what geological time period did the dinosaurs become extinct? (1)

....

(ii) How do scientists know that dinosaurs once lived on Earth? (1)

....

(c) What group of animals alive today is most closely related to the snake? (1)

....

(d) Which ancestor is shared by dinosaurs, crocodiles and the giant lizard, but is not an ancestor of tortoises? (1)

....

Variation and evolution

Module 32

For more help on this topic, see Letts GCSE Biology Revision Guide pages 74–75

1 Peppered moths are usually pale and speckled. They are often found amongst the lichens on silver birch tree bark. The data below estimates the average number of peppered moths spotted in a city centre before and after the Industrial Revolution.

Month	Before Industrial Revolution		After Industrial Revolution	
	Pale	Dark	Pale	Dark
June	1261	102	87	1035
July	1247	126	108	1336
August	1272	93	72	1019

(a) Complete the table by calculating the mean number of each colour of moth during the summer months. (2)

Before Industrial Revolution		After Industrial Revolution	
Pale	Dark	Pale	Dark
....	....	....	....

(b) Draw a bar graph to represent your results. (2)

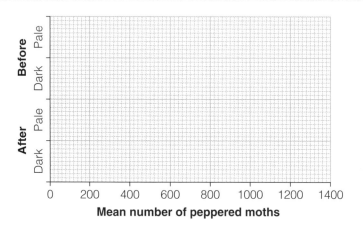

(c) Why do you think there were more pale-coloured moths than dark-coloured moths before the Industrial Revolution? (1)

....

(d) Explain why the number of dark-coloured peppered moths increased significantly during the Industrial Revolution. (2)

....

....

....

2 Lucy is an early hominid fossil that is 3.2 million years old. Why was this a significant find? (1)

....

For more help on this topic, see Letts GCSE Biology Revision Guide pages 76–77

1 From the box below, choose the correct words to complete these sentences. (2)

| selection | adapted | slow | genes | evolved |

Evolution suggests that all living things have .... from simple life forms developed billions of years ago. The process is .... and continual. Organisms that are better .... to their environment are more likely to survive. Adaptations are coded for by .... and can therefore be passed on to offspring.

2 Neo-Darwinists are scientists who have accepted Darwin's theory of natural selection but have built upon it with new ideas. They have developed the theory because of new evidence that has been found.

One of Darwin's main ideas was that successful characteristics can be passed on to the next generation. How might studies of inheritance have provided further evidence for this? (1)

....

....

3 **(a)** Cloning can occur naturally. Which type of cell division is involved in natural cloning? (1)

....

(b) Suggest why asexual reproduction could be useful to commercial plant growers. (2)

....

....

(c) Describe **two** disadvantages of commercial cloning. (2)

....

....

....

....

4 It is illegal to clone human embryos beyond 14 days old.
Suggest **one** reason why this is the case. (1)

....

....

For more help on this topic, see Letts GCSE Biology Revision Guide pages 78–79

1 (a) A sheep farmer wants to breed sheep that grow high quality wool. What four stages of selective breeding can he use to produce his desired variety? (3)

The first stage has been done for you.

1. Choose males and females that produce good quality wool.

2. ....

3. ....

4. ....

(b) Apart from high quality wool, name another characteristic that a farmer might want to selectively breed into his flock. (1)

....

2 Describe how genetic engineering is different from selective breeding. (2)

....

....

....

3 Explain the benefit of each of these examples of genetic engineering.

(a) Resistance to herbicide in soya plants (1)

....

....

(b) Inserting beta-carotene genes into rice plants (1)

....

....

4 Some people think that genetically engineering resistance to herbicides in plants could have unforeseen consequences. Give **one** example of a harmful effect. (1)

....

....

....

For more help on this topic, see Letts GCSE Biology Revision Guide pages 80–81

1. Lions, tigers and leopards are all carnivorous big cats. They have five toes on their front paws and four toes on their back paws. Their claws can be drawn back to avoid damage. They all roar. Tigers and leopards tend to be solitary animals but lions live in prides of females with one dominant male.

(a) Underline **one** piece of evidence from the information above that suggests that lions, tigers and leopards are all descended from a common ancestor. (1)

(b) This table shows how some scientists have named four species of large cat.

	Genus	Species
Lion	Panthera	leo
Tiger	Panthera	tigris
Leopard	Panthera	pardus
Snow leopard	Uncia	uncia

Are leopards more closely related to tigers or snow leopards? Explain your answer. (2)

....

....

....

2. Archaeopteryx is an ancient fossilised species of bird. When first discovered, scientists found it hard to classify.

Using features shown in the picture, explain why Archaeopteryx is difficult to classify. (2)

....

....

....

For more help on this topic, see Letts GCSE Biology Revision Guide pages 82–83

1 Complete the following passage about adaptations using words from the box below. (3)

environment	population	features	community	characteristics
survival	evolutionary	predatory	suited	

Adaptations are special .... or .... that make a living

organism particularly well .... to its .... Adaptations

are part of an .... process that increases a living organism's chance of

....

2 A new species of insectivorous mammal has been discovered in Borneo. It has been observed in rainforest undergrowth and more open savannah-like areas. Scientists have called the creature a *long-nosed batink*. They have studied its diet and obtained this data.

Food	Ants	Termites	Aphids	Beetles	Maggots	Bugs	Grubs
Mass eaten per day / g	275	380	320	75	150	20	110

(a) Plot the data for termites, beetles, bugs and grubs as a bar chart. (3)

(b) Calculate the percentage of the batink's diet that is made up from termites. Show your working. (2)

.... %

(c) From what you know about the batink, suggest **two** behavioural adaptations it might have that makes it successful. (2)

....

....

For more help on this topic, see Letts GCSE Biology Revision Guide pages 86–87

1 A meadow supports a wide variety of animals and plants. George is carrying out a survey of the meadow to assess the populations of organisms found there.

(a) State the term that describes the meadow as a place for organisms to live. (1)

....

(b) Which word describes the different populations in the meadow and their interaction with the physical factors found there? (1)

....

(c) George has laid pitfall traps in the meadow to capture and count soil invertebrates. He notices that there are many flying insects that are too difficult to count and identify.

Suggest an item of apparatus he could use to survey the flying insects. (1)

....

(d) George uses a 0.25 m² quadrat to survey the plant populations. He lays ten quadrats in one corner of the field and finds a mean count of 16 meadow buttercups per quadrat. He estimates the area of the meadow to be 5000 m².

Calculate the expected number of buttercups in the whole meadow.
Show your working. (2)

....

....

(e) George finds these two invertebrates in his pitfall traps.

Beetle   Snail

(i) The beetle feeds off other insects. Explain how a decrease in the number of beetles will eventually result in their numbers rising. (2)

....

....

(ii) Thrushes eat snails and worms. Describe what would happen to the number of snails if large numbers of thrushes arrived in their habitat. (1)

....

For more help on this topic, see Letts GCSE Biology Revision Guide pages 88–91

1 The diagram shows a digester that can make use of human sewage. The gas produced from this vessel contains a mixture of 60% methane and 40% carbon dioxide.

Gas trapped beneath metal gas holder

Gas release tap

Waste material

Residual 'digested' sludge

(a) What is the name of this type of biofuel? (1)

....

(b) Give **two** uses of this biofuel. (2)

1. ....

2. ....

(c) Explain why these types of digesters are useful in remote parts of the world. (1)

....

2 A group of students wanted to investigate factors affecting decay. They mixed soil with small discs cut from leaves. They divided the leaf disc / soil mixture equally into four test tubes, as shown below.

Muslin cloth

Leaf disc cut from leaf

Leaf discs and soil mixture

A	B	C	D
No added water 18°C	No added water 25°C	+10 ml water 18°C	+10 ml water 25°C

(a) In which tube would you expect the leaf discs to decay fastest? Give a reason for your answer. .... (2)

....

(b) The students did not add any microorganisms to the test tubes. Where will the microorganisms that cause decay come from? (1)

....

(c) Why did the students seal the tubes with muslin cloth instead of a rubber bung? (1)

....

(d) Suggest **one** way in which the students could use the leaf discs to measure the rate of decay. (1)

....

For more help on this topic, see Letts GCSE Biology Revision Guide pages 92–93

1 Circle the renewable resources. (1)

      water   minerals   oil   wind   coal   wood

2 Explain how rising average global temperatures may have an effect on the Earth.
Use the headings below to structure your answer. (3)

Climate zones around the world:

....

....

Sea levels:

....

....

Ice caps and glaciers:

....

....

3 At the moment, the human population is increasing exponentially.

(a) Sketch a graph that shows this increase. (2)

(b) On the *y*-axis, add a suitable unit for the population. (1)

(c) Suggest **two** reasons for this 'population explosion'. (2)

....

....

For more help on this topic, see Letts GCSE Biology Revision Guide page 94

1 In Ireland, four species of bumble bee are now endangered. Scientists are worried that numbers may become so low that they are inadequate to provide pollination to certain plants.

State **two** reasons why some organisms become endangered. (2)

....

....

2 **(a)** What is deforestation? Tick (✓) the correct definition. (1)

Planting new trees ☐

Forest fires caused by hot weather ☐

Cutting down large areas of forest ☐

Polluting national parks with litter ☐

(b) Which of the following is a consequence of deforestation? Tick (✓) the correct answer. (1)

Decrease in soil erosion in tropical regions ☐

Increase in atmospheric carbon dioxide ☐

Increase in average rainfall ☐

Increase in habitat area ☐

3 Other than using wood for timber, give **two** other reasons for large-scale deforestation. (2)

....

....

4 Circle the correct options in the sentences below. (6)

When deforestation occurs in **tropical / arctic / desert** regions, it has a devastating impact on the environment.

The loss of **trees / animals / insects** means less photosynthesis takes place, so less **oxygen / nitrogen / carbon dioxide** is removed from the atmosphere.

It also leads to a reduction in **variation / biodiversity / mutation**, because some species may become **protected / damaged / extinct** and **habitats / land / farms** are destroyed.

5 Sometimes when land has been cleared of forests to grow crops, farmers stop producing good yields after a few years. Explain why. (1)

....

....

For more help on this topic, see Letts GCSE Biology Revision Guide page 95

1 The picture shows the energy intake and use for a cow.

(a) What type of energy does the cow's intake consist of? Tick (✓) the correct answer. (1)

2000 kJ used by the cow for other purposes

6000 kJ intake

New growth

3000 kJ in faeces

Chemical energy ☐   Potential energy ☐

Light energy ☐   Heat energy ☐

(b) Using the formula below, calculate the energy efficiency for the cow. Show your working. (2)

$$\text{energy efficiency} = \frac{\text{energy used usefully for new growth}}{\text{total energy taken in}} \times 100\%$$

....

....

(c) Humans do not need to eat as much biomass as cows do. Explain why. (2)

....

....

(d) Use your responses to (b) and (c) to explain why eating cereals and grains is more energy-efficient than eating meat. In your answer, explain the implications for agricultural land use if significant numbers of a population are vegetarian. (6)

....

....

....

....

....

....

....

....

....

For more help on this topic, see Letts GCSE Biology Revision Guide pages 96–97

1. Some scientists studied the numbers of cod caught in cool to temperate waters in the northern hemisphere. They obtained the following data, which is expressed in a graph.

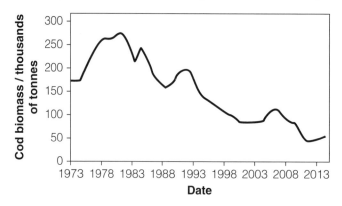

(a) What was the estimated cod biomass in 1988? (1)

.... thousand tonnes

(b) Describe the change in cod numbers between 1988 and 2013. (2)

....

....

(c) International fishing quotas are set in order to manage the numbers of fish in our seas. The table shows data about fishing quotas set by an international fishing commission.

Fish species	UK quota 2013 / tonnes	UK quota 2014 / tonnes
Cod	11 216	13 123
Haddock	27 507	23 381
Whiting	8426	3287

(i) By how much did the cod quota change between 2013 and 2014? (1)

.... tonnes

(ii) Suggest possible reasons for the decreased quota for haddock. (2)

....

....

(d) Suggest **one** other measure that fisheries councils could take to prevent over-fishing. (1)

....

For more help on this topic, see Letts GCSE Biology Revision Guide pages 98–99

GCSE (9–1)
Biology
Paper 1

Higher tier

Time: 1 hour 45 minutes

You may use:

- a calculator
- a ruler.

Instructions

- Use black ink or black ball-point pen. Draw diagrams in pencil.
- Read each question carefully before you start to write your answer.
- Answer **all** questions in the spaces provided.
- Show your working in any calculator question and include units in your answer where appropriate.
- In questions marked with an asterisk (*), marks will be awarded for your ability to structure your answer logically, showing how the points that you make are related or follow on from each other where appropriate.

Information

- The marks for each question are shown in brackets.
  Use this as a guide to how much time to spend on each question.
- The maximum mark for this paper is 100.
- Diagrams are not accurately drawn unless otherwise stated.

Name: ....

1 **(a)** Which substance is a product of anaerobic respiration in humans? Tick (✓) **one** box. **[1]**

Carbon dioxide ☐

Ethanol ☐

Glucose ☐

Lactic acid ☐

(b) Which substance is a product of aerobic respiration in plants? Tick (✓) **one** box. **[1]**

Carbon dioxide ☐

Ethanol ☐

Glucose ☐

Lactic acid ☐

2

Figure 1

(a) Niamh in **Figure 1** is training for a marathon. Every few days she runs a long distance. This builds up the number of mitochondria in her muscle cells.

What is the advantage for Niamh of having extra mitochondria in her muscle cells?
Tick (✓) **one** box. **[1]**

Her muscles become stronger. ☐

Her muscles can contract faster. ☐

Her muscles can release more energy. ☐

Her muscles can repair faster after injury. ☐

*(b) Bob in **Figure 2** has been running hard and has an oxygen debt. Describe what causes an oxygen debt after a session of vigorous exercise and how Bob can recover from its effects. **[3]**

Figure 2

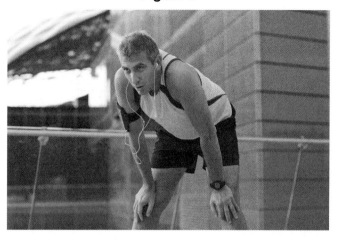

....

....

....

....

*(c) Tariq is competing in a 10-mile running race. His heart rate and breathing rate increase. Describe how this helps his muscles during the race. **[3]**

....

....

....

3 Which of the following structures are in the correct size order, starting with the smallest? Tick (✓) **one** box. **[1]**

cell, tissue, organ, system ☐

tissue, organ, system, cell ☐

cell, organ, system, tissue ☐

tissue, system, cell, organ ☐

4 Which part of the blood helps protect the body from pathogens? Tick (✓) **one** box. **[1]**

Plasma ☐

Platelets ☐

Red blood cells ☐

White blood cells ☐

5 (a) From which section of the human heart is blood pumped to the lungs?
Tick (✓) **one** box. **[1]**

Left atrium ☐

Right atrium ☐

Left ventricle ☐

Right ventricle ☐

(b) Explain why the left side of the heart is more muscular than the right side. **[1]**

....

....

(c) The heart contains a number of valves.

Describe how the valves help the heart pump blood more effectively. **[1]**

....

....

(d) There are around 105 650 deaths in the UK from smoking-related causes each year. The number of deaths due to cardiovascular disease that is linked to smoking is estimated to be 22 100.

What percentage of deaths from smoking each year is due to cardiovascular disease? Show your working. Give your answer to two significant figures. **[2]**

....

(e) The chance of heart disease can be reduced by lowering alcohol intake and by not smoking. Write about **two** other choices that can be made to reduce the chance of heart disease. **[2]**

....

....

6 (a) Explain how skin defends the human body against disease. **[2]**

....

....

(b) Disease can be caused by bacteria. Bacteria multiply very quickly – the numbers of cholera bacteria can double every 20 minutes.

Ten cholera bacteria were kept in ideal conditions for growth. How many cholera bacteria were there after two hours? Show your working. **[2]**

....

....

(c) Explain why measles cannot be treated with antibiotics. **[2]**

....

....

(d) Figure 3 shows a photomicrograph of the bacterium *E. coli*, which is a common cause of stomach upsets. The magnification of the photo is × 5000.

Figure 3

The average magnified length of the bacteria shown in **Figure 3** is 10 mm. Calculate the actual length of an *E. coli* bacterium in µm (1 µm = 1×10^{-3} mm). Show your working. **[2]**

....

....

(e) The spread of cholera is often a problem in temporary refugee camps. One way cholera is spread is through contaminated water.

What simple measures can be taken to reduce the spread of cholera in the camps? **[2]**

....

....

(f) If a disease is infectious, an epidemic can be prevented by vaccination.

Explain why a very high percentage of the population need to be vaccinated for the prevention to be successful. **[2]**

....

....

7 Which of the following is found in a plant cell but not in an animal cell?
Tick (✓) **one** box.   **[1]**

Cell membrane   ☐

Cytoplasm   ☐

Nucleus   ☐

Cell wall   ☐

*| **8** Describe the aseptic method used to grow a colony of bacteria cells from pond water using a sterilised petri dish containing nutrient agar jelly.   **[4]**

....

....

....

....

9 Human stem cell research could lead to new treatments for conditions such as diabetes.

(a) Outline **two** reasons why some people think that human stem cell research should not be allowed.   **[2]**

....

....

(b) Look at **Figure 4**. What is the name of the process by which a stem cell becomes a new cell type?   **[1]**

Figure 4

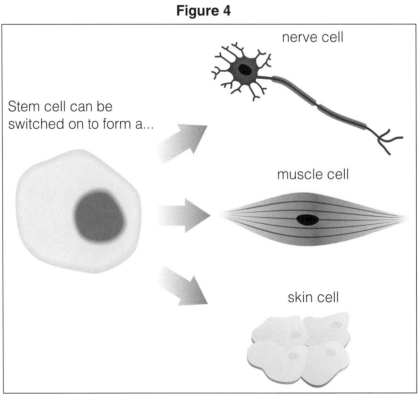

....

10 **(a)** Stomata are found on the underside of a plant leaf. During the day the stomata open to allow carbon dioxide into the leaf. Outline how the stomata open. **[2]**

....

....

(b) Carbon dioxide moves into a leaf by diffusion. Describe the process of diffusion. **[2]**

....

....

11 **(a)** **Figure 5** shows a celery plant. The stalk of a celery plant contains xylem vessels.

Figure 5

Describe the structure of xylem vessels. **[2]**

....

....

(b) Describe how root cells are adapted to allow the efficient absorption of water. **[2]**

....

....

12 **Figure 6** shows an experiment to investigate how water is taken up by a plant.

Figure 6

Layer of oil

Water

(a) What is the purpose of the layer of oil? **[1]**

....

(b) Table 1 shows the results of the experiment.

Table 1

Time (days)	0	1	2	3	4
Volume of water in cylinder (cm³)	50	47	43	42	40

Calculate the average water loss per day from the measuring cylinder in **Figure 6**.
Show your working. **[2]**

....

....

Average water loss: .... cm³ per day

13 **Figure 7** shows a sheepdog puppy. There are 39 pairs of chromosomes in the skin cell of a sheepdog puppy. Two of the chromosomes determine the sex of the puppy.

Figure 7

(a) How many chromosomes are there in the sperm cell of a sheepdog? Tick (✓) **one** box. **[1]**

39 ☐

76 ☐

78 ☐

80 ☐

(b) The number of skin cells increases as the puppy grows.

A skin cell grows and then divides into two skin cells. What is the name of this process?
Explain why each skin cell has the same number of chromosomes. **[4]**

....

....

....

....

14 Genetically engineered bacteria can be used to make human insulin to treat diabetes. The human genes to make insulin are inserted into the bacteria DNA.

Outline **three** reasons why bacteria are chosen for this process. **[3]**

....

....

....

15 In a recent newspaper article, the following statement appeared:

You can only get cancer if you have the wrong genes.

This is not true.

Write down **three** other factors that could be involved in the formation of cancer cells. **[3]**

....

....

....

16 **(a)** Which of the following substances breaks down starch during digestion?
Tick (✓) **one** box. **[1]**

Amylase ☐

Cellulose ☐

Lipase ☐

Protease ☐

*(b) Describe the simple chemical steps that convert plant protein in your diet into a human protein such as collagen. **[4]**

....

....

....

....

(c) A new biological washing powder (see **Figure 8**) contains protease and lipase enzymes. It is very good at removing food stains from clothing in a 30 °C wash.

Figure 8

Explain why the washing powder is less effective when used in a 60 °C wash. **[2]**

....

....

17 Plants and animals use glucose for respiration. Plants also convert glucose into different substances. Name **three** of these substances and give a reason why each one is important. **[3]**

....

....

....

18 **Figure 9** shows an experiment to demonstrate osmosis.

Figure 9

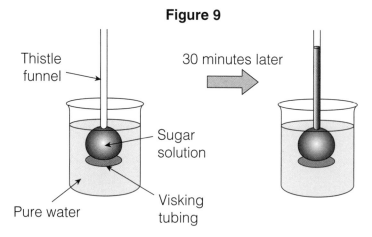

Explain why the volume of solution inside the thistle funnel has increased. **[3]**

....

....

....

*19 Black spot is a fungal disease that affects rose leaves (see **Figure 10**). Fatima has noticed that roses growing in areas with high air pollution are less affected by the disease. She thinks that regular exposure to acid rain is stopping the disease from developing.

Figure 10

Describe a simple experiment that Fatima could carry out to test her theory. [3]

....

....

....

....

20 The foxglove plant contains toxic substances that, if eaten, cause the heart to slow down or even stop. What is the benefit to the plant of being poisonous? [1]

....

21 (a) A farmer has tested the soil in one of his fields and found that it does not have enough nitrate content for his next crop. What will be the effect on his crop if he does nothing about it? [1]

....

(b) The farmer researches what type of manure he could use on his field. He only wants to use manure that comes from his own farm animals. **Table 2** shows his findings.

Table 2

Animal	Cow	Horse	Poultry	Rabbit
Percentage of nitrate in manure	0.7	0.8	2.1	2.0
Number of animals on the farm	120	5	220	35

Outline **one** advantage and **one** disadvantage of using rabbit manure on the field. [2]

....

....

22 **(a)** Thomas burns paraffin in a small stove inside his greenhouse during March and April.
How does this benefit the growth of his greenhouse plants? **[2]**

....

....

(b) Complete the balanced symbol equation for photosynthesis. **[2]**

$$6\ CO_2\ +\ ....\ \longrightarrow\ C_6H_{12}O_6\ +\ ....$$

*(c) Anoushka investigates the effect of light on photosynthesis at 25 °C.
She uses the apparatus shown in **Figure 11**.

Figure 11

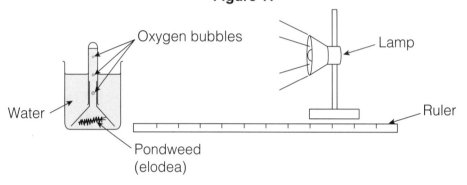

She moves the lamp and counts the bubbles at different distances from the pondweed.
Table 3 shows her results.

Table 3

Distance from lamp to pondweed (cm)	Number of bubbles counted in five minutes
10	241
20	124
30	60
40	36
50	24

Describe the pattern in the results in **Table 3** and predict how the pattern would change if the experiment was repeated at 35 °C and at 55 °C. Explain your answers. **[6]**

....

....

....

....

....

....

....

....

....

....

23 **Figure 12** shows the antigens of a pathogen.

Figure 12

A   B   C   D

(a) Look at images A–D, which show the binding site of four Y-shaped antibodies. Which antibody will the body make to protect itself from the disease caused by the pathogen?
Tick (✓) **one** box. **[1]**

A ☐

B ☐

C ☐

D ☐

(b) A vaccine contains the pathogen that causes the disease. Explain why the patient does not develop the disease when being treated with a vaccine. **[1]**

....

24 Outline why it is difficult to develop drugs that disable or destroy viruses. **[2]**

....

....

25 The development of certain types of breast cancer are aided by the over production in the body of a particular enzyme called HER2.

A drug containing a monoclonal antibody has been developed that reduces the activity of HER2 in the body.

***(a)** Explain how the drug reduces the activity of the enzyme in the patient. **[3]**

....

....

....

....

(b) When this drug went to the clinical trial stage of testing, it was tested in a 'double blind' trial.

Describe how a 'double blind' trial is carried out and explain why it is more effective than a simple blind trial. **[3]**

....

....

....

....

TOTAL FOR PAPER = 100 MARKS

GCSE (9–1)
Biology
Paper 2

Higher tier

Time: 1 hour 45 minutes

You may use:

- a calculator
- a ruler.

Instructions

- Use black ink or black ball-point pen. Draw diagrams in pencil.
- Read each question carefully before you start to write your answer.
- Answer **all** questions in the spaces provided.
- Show your working in any calculator question and include units in your answer where appropriate.
- In questions marked with an asterisk (*), marks will be awarded for your ability to structure your answer logically, showing how the points that you make are related or follow on from each other where appropriate.

Information

- The marks for each question are shown in brackets.
  Use this as a guide to how much time to spend on each question.
- The maximum mark for this paper is 100.
- Diagrams are not accurately drawn unless otherwise stated.

Name: _____

1 **Figure 1** shows a simple food chain. The arrows represent the transfer of energy in the food chain.

Figure 1

Sun   A →   Grass   B →   Rabbit   C →   Stoat   D →   Fox

Which arrow shows the greatest transfer of energy?
Tick (✓) **one** box.   **[1]**

A ☐

B ☐

C ☐

D ☐

2 **Figure 2** shows a flock of seagulls. The number of seagulls in a flock is affected by both abiotic and biotic factors.

Figure 2

Which of the following is a biotic factor?
Tick (✓) **one** box.   **[1]**

Temperature ☐

Rainfall ☐

Disease ☐

Ocean tides ☐

3 Polar bears live in the Arctic. As **Figure 3** shows, they are often found on ice floes where they hunt seals.

Figure 3

Describe **two** adaptations that help polar bears survive in the arctic wilderness. **[2]**

....

....

4 An ecologist surveys a meadow to determine the number of field voles living there.

Humane traps are set and after 8 hours, 15 voles have been captured.

Each vole is marked by shaving a small section of fur from its back and is then released.

The traps are set again.

After a further 8 hours, 21 voles are captured. Four of these have shaved backs.

Use this formula to calculate the number of field voles in the meadow:

$$\frac{\text{number in first sample} \times \text{number in second sample}}{\text{number in second sample previously marked}}$$

Show your working. **[2]**

....

....

5 **(a)** Most of the salmon sold in supermarkets comes from fish farms. The salmon are raised in large cages containing thousands of salmon.

Outline **one** advantage and **one** problem of using this method of farming fish. **[2]**

....

....

(b) Fish farming is seen as a sustainable method of providing fish for the table. Due to overfishing, 'wild' fish stocks are declining quickly.

Describe what measures are now being taken to preserve 'wild' fish stocks. **[2]**

....

....

6 **Figure 4** shows a kakapo (*Strigops habroptilus*), which is a flightless parrot found only on a few small islands in New Zealand.

Figure 4

(a) Using the Linnaean system, what is the genus of the Kakapo? Tick (✓) **one** box. **[1]**

Animalia ☐

Aves ☐

Strigops ☐

habroptilus ☐

(b) The kakapo is a herbivore. It lives in woodland and is an excellent tree climber.

What part does the kakapo play in the woodland ecosystem? Tick (✓) **one** box. **[1]**

Decomposer ☐

Primary consumer ☐

Producer ☐

Secondary consumer ☐

(c) The kakapo has been threatened with extinction for over one hundred years. It has become an endangered species since Europeans brought animals such as cats, dogs and rats into New Zealand.

Use ideas about genetics to explain why it has not evolved to escape from new predators. **[3]**

....

....

....

7 The following text is one of the instructions on a packet of antibiotic tablets (see **Figure 5**):
Complete the prescribed course of treatment as directed by your doctor.

Figure 5

Explain why this instruction is important to stop bacteria becoming resistant to this antibiotic. **[3]**

....

....

....

8 Why are fossils only found in sedimentary rocks? **[1]**

....

....

9 Outline **two** reasons why Darwin's theory of evolution took many years to gain acceptance by the scientific community. **[2]**

....

....

10 What activity is the cerebellum area of the brain associated with?
Tick (✓) **one** box. **[1]**

Control of breathing ☐

Consciousness ☐

Memory ☐

Control of movement ☐

11 **Figure 6** shows some of the endocrine system.

Figure 6

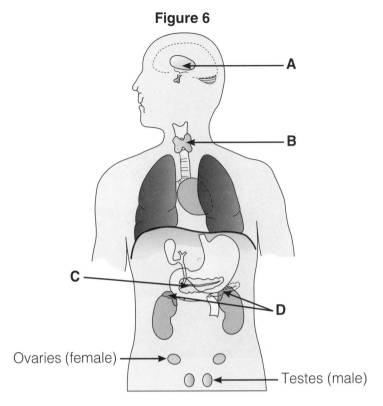

Ovaries (female)

Testes (male)

Which label shows the adrenal gland?
Tick (✓) **one** box. [1]

A ☐

B ☐

C ☐

D ☐

*12 A sauna is a very hot, small, wooden room, typically heated to above 80°C (see **Figure 7**). Sitting in a sauna is good for relaxing muscles and helps to cleanse the skin.

Figure 7

In Finland people sit in a sauna for up to 20 minutes and then go outside and plunge into icy cold water.

Describe how the body responds to heating up in the sauna and the changes that happen as it cools rapidly in icy cold water. **[4]**

....

....

....

....

*13 **Figure 8** is an illustration of an eye starting to look at a very bright object in the distance.

Figure 8

Changes happen inside the eye to get a focused image that does not appear too bright. How will muscles in the eye make these changes? **[4]**

....

....

....

....

14 **Figure 9** shows a mango. Mangoes are tropical fruits that are exported all over the world. They are picked early and ripened when they reach the UK.

Figure 9

Which method is used to ripen the fruit? Tick (✓) **one** box. **[1]**

Stored in an atmosphere of carbon dioxide gas ☐

Sprayed with a solution of the hormone auxin ☐

Stored in an atmosphere of ethene gas ☐

Sprayed with a solution of the hormone gibberellin ☐

15 **Figure 10** shows a broad bean seed five days after germination.

Figure 10

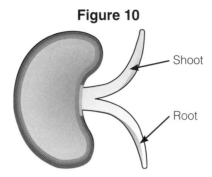

Shoot

Root

(a) Describe and explain how the shoot responds to gravity. **[3]**

....

....

....

(b) The root grows in the opposite direction. Describe how auxin behaves in the root. **[2]**

....

....

16 Two students carried out an experiment to investigate the decay of grass cuttings.

• They put the cuttings in three different-coloured plastic bags – each bag had a few very small holes for ventilation.

• The bags were placed together at the edge of the school field.

• The bags were weighed at the start of the experiment and again three months later.

Table 1 shows the results.

Table 1

	Black bag (A)	Yellow bag (B)	White bag (C)
Mass of bag and grass cuttings at the start (g)	320.4	350.6	325.7
Mass of bag and grass cuttings after three months (g)	271.7	305.7	290.9
% decrease in mass	15.2	12.8	10.7

(a) Predict the percentage decrease in mass if the experiment is repeated with a dark brown bag. Explain your answer. **[3]**

....

....

....

(b) Putting the three bags in the same place on the school field is controlling a variable. Suggest **two** other control variables to help improve this experiment. [2]

1. ....

2. ....

17 The reaction times of six people were measured.

They put on headphones and were asked to push a button when they heard a sound. The button was connected to a timer.

Table 2 shows the results.

Table 2

Person	Gender	Reaction time in seconds				
		1	2	3	4	5
A	Male	0.26	0.25	0.27	0.25	0.27
B	Female	0.25	0.25	0.26	0.22	0.24
C	Male	0.31	1.43	0.32	0.29	0.32
D	Female	0.22	0.23	0.25	0.22	0.23
E	Male	0.27	0.31	0.30	0.28	0.26
F	Female	0.23	0.19	0.21	0.21	0.22

(a) Describe a pattern in these results. [1]

....

(b) Calculate the mean reaction time for person C, ignoring any outliers. Show your working. [2]

....

....

(c) When person D was concentrating on the test, someone touched her arm and she jumped. Her response was a reflex action. What are the **two** main features of a reflex action? [2]

....

....

*(d) A reflex action involves a 'message' travelling along a sensory neurone as an electrical impulse. The electrical impulse reaches a junction called a synapse.

Describe what happens at the synapse for the 'message' to continue its journey. [4]

....

....

....

....

18 Neuroscientists have linked particular areas of the brain to different functions.

Outline **one** technique used to map the brain and discuss an ethical issue associated with it. **[2]**

....

....

19 **Figure 11** shows hormone levels in a woman's bloodstream during her menstrual cycle.

Figure 11

————— FSH   - - - - Oestrogen   ■■■■ Progesterone   ——— LH

(a) The woman believes that her best chance of becoming pregnant is after day 21 of the cycle. Is she correct? Use the levels of hormones in **Figure 11** to explain your answer. **[2]**

....

....

....

(b) What is the role of progesterone in the menstrual cycle? **[2]**

....

....

(c) Explain how the hormones used in oral contraceptives prevent conception. **[2]**

....

....

(d) Fertility drugs have helped many couples have children, where previously they could not. However, the process is not without its problems.

Outline **two** problems with this type of treatment. **[2]**

....

....

20 **Figure 12** shows four methods of plant reproduction.

Figure 12

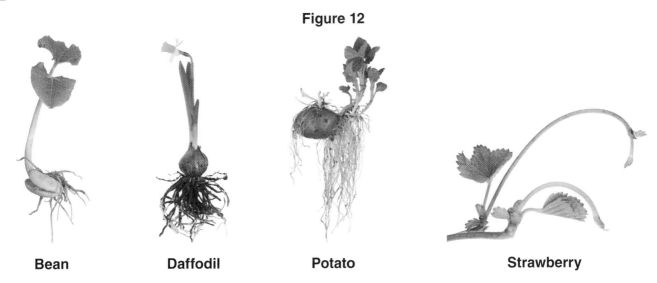

| Bean | Daffodil | Potato | Strawberry |

Which method shows plant reproduction with the greatest genetic variation?
Tick (✓) **one** box. [1]

Bean plant from seed ☐

Daffodil plant from bulb ☐

Potato plant from tuber ☐

Strawberry plant from runner ☐

21 **Figure 13** shows the three stages involved in tissue culturing.

Figure 13

Outline **one** benefit and **one** disadvantage of this method of plant cultivation. [2]

....

....

*22 A farmer keeps two different herds of cows. The two types of cow are shown in **Figure 14**.

Figure 14

Herd 1

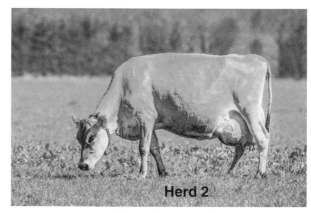
Herd 2

- Each cow in herd 1 produces a high volume of low fat milk.

- Each cow in herd 2 produces small amounts of high cream milk.

The farmer wants to modify his milk yield to get high volumes of creamy milk. He can sell the creamy milk to local ice-cream makers.

Describe how the farmer can use selective breeding to achieve his aim.   [4]

....

....

....

....

23 Selective breeding methods have recently been used to produce vegetables that, when eaten, help reduce cholesterol levels in humans.

If the vegetables had been produced by genetic engineering, some people may be worried about them being used for human consumption. Give **two** reasons why.   [2]

....

....

....

24 (a) Which term describes different versions of the same gene?
        Tick (✓) **one** box.   [1]

    Variant   ☐

    Dominant   ☐

    Recessive   ☐

    Allele   ☐

(b) Figure 15 shows Max and Sharon with their three children: Dylan, Emily and Georgina.

Figure 15

Max   Sharon

Dylan   Emily   Georgina

Which members of the family share the most genes? Tick (✓) **one** box.   **[1]**

Dylan and Max   ☐

Emily and Sharon   ☐

Emily and Georgina   ☐

Georgina and Max   ☐

25 **(a)** DNA contains four bases: G, C, A and T.

There are the same number of G bases as C bases. There are also the same number of A bases as T bases.

The analysis of one strand of DNA found that 27% was composed of base T. Calculate the percentage of the other three bases. Show your working.   **[3]**

....

....

....

(b) The compounds that form the 'rungs' on the DNA ladder and code for the structure of a protein are arranged in pairs.

Figure 16 shows a diagram of DNA. One strand has been filled in.

Figure 16

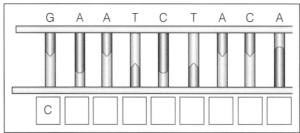

Enter the matching compounds in the boxes. [1]

(c) How many amino acids are coded by the section of DNA shown in **Figure 16**?
Explain your answer. [3]

....

....

....

26 Cystic fibrosis is a genetic disorder. Adam has the disorder but his mother and father did not show signs of the condition.

(a) Complete the Punnett diagram to show how this could occur. Use f as the allele for cystic fibrosis. [2]

(b) Before Adam was conceived, what was the probability that his parents would have a child with cystic fibrosis? [1]

....

(c) Which phrase describes the genotype of Adam's parents? [1]

....

*27 (a) Diabetes is a condition where the body cannot control the level of glucose in the blood.

Describe how the human body normally controls the level of glucose in the blood and how people with type 1 and type 2 diabetes maintain the correct levels of glucose in the blood. **[6]**

....

....

....

....

....

....

....

....

....

(b) Diabetes can adversely affect the kidneys.

Kidneys remove urea from the bloodstream. Outline what other jobs the kidneys do. **[2]**

....

....

(c) A person with kidney disease must control their diet to reduce the kidneys' workload.

Explain in detail why the amount of protein in the diet must be limited. **[4]**

....

....

....

....

....

28 Large areas of Amazon rainforest are cleared to provide land for farming every year. Explain how deforestation is linked to global warming. **[2]**

....

....

....

29 Write down **two** reasons why biodiversity is important. **[2]**

....

....

30 Modern sustainable farming methods can provide enough food for the human population. Explain the meaning of the phrase 'sustainable farming'. **[1]**

....

TOTAL FOR PAPER = 100 MARKS

Answers

CELL BIOLOGY

Page 4

1. (a) Nucleus **(1)**
   (b) Mitochondria are too small to see with a light microscope / require an electron microscope / resolution of microscope not high enough. **(1)**
   (c) Liver cells require the release of a lot of energy **(1)**; mitochondria release energy for muscle contraction **(1)**.
   (d) Cell, cytoplasm, nucleus, chromosome, gene **(2 marks for everything in the correct order, 1 mark if cell, cytoplasm and nucleus are in the correct order, reading left to right)**

2. (a) Bacteria have a chromosomal loop; have plasmids; no nuclear membrane / nucleus. **(1)**
   (b) Prokaryotic ✓ **(1)**

Page 5

1. (a) An undifferentiated cell that can develop into one of many different types. **(1)**
   (b) **Any two from:** nucleus, cytoplasm, cell / plasma membrane, mitochondria, ribosomes. **(2)**

2. (a) **Any two from:** therapeutic cloning, treating paralysis, repairing nerve damage, cancer research, grow new organs for transplantation. **(2)**
   (b) **Any one from:** stem cells are sometimes obtained from human embryos and people believe it is wrong to use embryos for this purpose, risk of viral infections. **(1)**

3. $\frac{3600}{30} \times 200$ **(1)** = 24 000 µm **(1)** = 24 mm **(1)**

Page 6

1. (a) Line should point to one of the objective lenses / rotating nose cone. **(1)**
   (b) The organelles are too small to see **(1)** / microscope doesn't have a high enough resolving power. **(1)**
   (c) Size of real object = $\frac{3}{400}$ **(1)** = 0.0075 cm **(1)** = 75 µm **(1)**

2. (a) Scanning electron microscope **(1)**
   (b) **For 2 marks, accept any answer between 80–100 minutes;** if answer is incorrect, award 1 mark for the idea that there have been 4 divisions.

Page 7

1. **Any two from:** specialised organs carry out a specific job; multicellular organisms are complex and require specialised organs so they can grow larger; single-celled organisms are small enough not to require specialised cells and transport systems. **(2)**

2.

Mitosis	Meiosis
Involved in asexual reproduction	**Involved in sexual reproduction (1)**
Produces clones / no variation (1)	Produces variation
Produces cells with 46 chromosomes	**Produces cells with 23 chromosomes (1)**

3. (a) Meiosis **(1)**
   (b) Four cells produced (in second meiotic division) **(1)**

4. **Top label:** New bases pair up with exposed bases on each strand **(1)**; **bottom label:** Two identical strands of DNA / double helices formed **(1)**.

Page 8

1. $C_6H_{12}O_6 + 6O_2 \longrightarrow 6CO_2 + 6H_2O$ **(1 mark for correct formulae, 1 mark for correct balancing)**

2. (a) **Any two from:** larger athletes will use more oxygen due to their higher muscle mass; the adjustment allows rates to be fairly / accurately compared; different athletes may have different masses. **(2)**
   (b) Sprinting has a greater energy demand **(1)**, so more oxygen is needed **(1)**.

(c) Boris' consumption rate would be lower **(1)** because his lungs, heart and muscles are less efficient at transporting / using oxygen **(1)**.

Page 9

1. (a)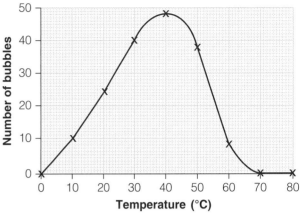
   (2 marks for correct plotting; 1 mark for smooth curve; subtract 1 mark for every incorrect plot)
   (b) The rate of bubbles produced increases until it reaches an optimum / maximum **(1)**; then it decreases rapidly, producing no bubbles at 70°C **(1)**.
   (c) 40°C **(1)**
   (d) **Any two from:** enzyme / active site has changed shape / become denatured; substrate / hydrogen peroxide no longer fits active site, so substrate cannot be broken down; low pH of the stomach **or** amylase works best at alkaline pH and stomach is acid. **(2)**

TRANSPORT SYSTEMS AND PHOTOSYNTHESIS

Page 10

1. (a) **Any two named small nutrient molecules**, e.g. glucose, vitamins, minerals, ions, amino acids, oxygen **(2)**.
   (b) **Any one from:** carbon dioxide or urea. **(1)**

2. (a) Water moves down concentration gradient from high water concentration to low water concentration **(1)**, across a partially / differentially permeable membrane / plasma membrane **(1)**; gradient maintained by input and output of water at each end of cell line **(1)**.
   (b) Water moving from plant cell to plant cell ✓ **(1)**; A pear losing water in a concentrated solution of sugar ✓ **(1)**; Water moving from blood plasma to body cells ✓ **(1)**.

3. (a) Rhubarb cells turgid **(1)**; because water moves into cells due to osmosis **(1)**.
   (b) **Any two from:** plasmolysed; plant cell vacuole extremely small; membrane pulled away from wall. **(2)**

Page 11

1. **From top: (a)** (upper) epidermis **(1)**; **(b)** spongy layer / mesophyll **(1)**; **(c)** air space **(1)**.

2. **Roots:** anchor plant in soil / absorb water and minerals **(1)**
   Stem: supports leaves and flowers, transports substances up and down the plant **(1)**
   Leaf: organs of photosynthesis **(1)**
   Flower: reproductive organs, formation of seeds **(1)**

3. **Any three from:** dead cells without cytoplasm; no end walls; hollow lumen; continuous tubes – all adaptations allow efficient movement of water in columns. **(3)**

4. (a) **Any one from:** phloem have perforated end walls / xylem has no end wall; xylem have hard cell walls (contain lignin) / phloem have soft cell walls. **(1)**
   (b) Aphids extract / eat sugar **(1)**; sugar solution transported in phloem **(1)**.

Page 12

1. (a) $\frac{8}{43} \times 100 = 18.6\%$ **(1 mark for calculation, 1 mark for correct answer)**
    (b) B (cold moving air) **(1)**
    (c) Water column in xylem would move upwards / towards the leaves more quickly. **(1)**

2. **This is a model answer, which would score the full 6 marks:** As light intensity increases during the day, the rate of photosynthesis increases in the guard cells. This results in more sugar being manufactured, which raises the solute concentration. Increased potassium ions contribute to increased solute concentration too. The guard cells therefore draw in water from surrounding cells by osmosis, becoming more turgid. This causes the stoma to become wider. The arrangement of cellulose in the cell walls of the guard cells means that there is more expansion in the outer wall, resulting in a wider stoma.

Page 13

1. (a) (i) Scotland **(1)**
        (ii) 50 deaths per 100 000 (210 – 160) **(1)**
    (b) Men have higher death rates than women. **(1)**

2. Artery – 3 **(1)**; Capillaries in the body – 4 **(1)**; Vein – 1 **(1)**; Capillaries in the lungs – 2 **(1)**

Page 14

1. (a) 924.5 **(2)**; **if the answer is incorrect then showing the working (926 + 923 = 1849, then $\frac{1849}{2}$) will gain 1 mark**
    (b) Rats have different body masses / to standardise results. **(1)**
    (c) As the warfarin dose increases, the time to clot also increases. **(1)**

2. Agree **(1)** because as vital capacity increases the time underwater also increases **(1)**.
    Or disagree **(1)** due to **any one from**: only five subjects / not enough data; need to find divers with higher / lower vital capacities **(1)**.

Page 15

1. (a)

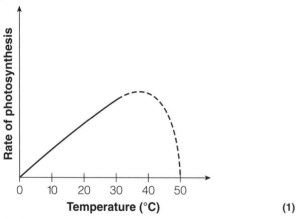

    (b) As the temperature increases, the rate of photosynthesis increases due to more rapid molecular movement and therefore more frequent successful collisions between molecules **(1)**. By 40 °C, the rate peaks and beyond this point enzymes controlling photosynthesis become denatured and the reaction stops **(1)**.

2. (a) Leaves **(1)**
    (b) **Cellulose:** cell walls for support **(1)**; **Protein:** growth / cell membranes / enzyme production **(1)**.
    (c) carbon dioxide + water ⟶ glucose + oxygen
        (1 mark for reactants, 1 mark for products)

3. (a) **Any two from:** the increased temperature from the stove will increase photosynthesis rate; increased carbon dioxide concentration will have the same effect; increased photosynthesis means increased starch production / yield. **(2)**
    (b) **Any one from:** increase light regime, e.g. artificial lighting switched on at night time; increased light intensity / brighter lights. **(1)**

HEALTH, DISEASE AND THE DEVELOPMENT OF MEDICINES

Page 16

1. (a) 13.8–14.8% **(1)**
    (b) Glycogen **(1)** found in liver / muscles **(1)**
    (c) **Any two from:** heart disease / CVD / stroke; cancer; diabetes; asthma / eczema / autoimmune diseases; poor nutrition – named example, e.g. rickets; genetic conditions, e.g. cystic fibrosis; eating disorders, e.g. anorexia; mental health conditions; alcoholism / addiction; named inherited disease. **(2)**

2. (a) ×20 **(1)**
    (b) **Any one from:** low birth weight; premature birth; higher risk of still birth. **(1)**

Page 17

1. (a) Pathogen **(1)**
    (b) Cause cell damage **(1)**; the toxins produced damage tissues. **(1)**

2. (a) **Any two from:** diarrhoea; vomiting; dehydration. **(2)**
    (b) Cholera spread by drinking contaminated water **(1)**; water easily contaminated because water supply / sewage systems damaged **or** overcrowding and poor hygiene in disaster zones **(1)**.

3. (a) **Any two from:** malaria is transmitted by the mosquito; warm temperatures are ideal for mosquitos to thrive; stagnant water is an ideal habitat for mosquito eggs to be laid / larvae to survive **(2)**.
    (b) **Mosquito:** vector **(1)**
        Plasmodium: parasite **(1)**
    (c) Nets will deter mosquitoes / prevent bites / prevent transferral of plasmodium **(1)**; antivirals are ineffective as plasmodium is a protist / not a virus **(1)**.

Page 18

1. (a) Antibodies **(1)**
    (b) Pathogens are clumped together to prevent their further reproduction, to make them easier for phagocytes to digest. **(1)**
    (c)

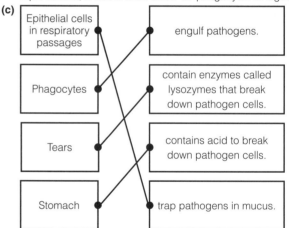

    (1 mark for each correct line up to 3 marks, subtract 1 mark for any additional lines)

2. (a) **Any one from:** droplet infection / coughing / sneezing / water droplets in breath / aerosol. **(1)**
    (b) Answer in the range 16–17 days **(1)**
    (c) 9 arbitrary units **(1)** (9.5 – 0.5) **(1)**
    (d) Memory cells recognise future invasion of pathogen **(1)**; they can produce the necessary antibodies much quicker, and at higher levels, if the same pathogen is detected again **(1)**.

Page 19

1. **This is a model answer, which would score the full 6 marks:** HIV proteins can be triggered and manufactured in existing human cells. The genes that code for the viral proteins are injected into the bloodstream. An adenovirus shell prevents them from being destroyed by the body's general defences. Once inside a cell, the genes instruct it to produce viral proteins that are presented at the cell surface membrane. The body's lymphocytes then recognise these antigens and produce antibodies against them. Memory cells sensitive to the viral proteins are then stored in case the body is exposed to the antigens again.

2. **Accept any three from:** Bacteria are becoming resistant to many modern antibiotics; doctors have in the past over-prescribed antibiotics; mutations in bacteria have led to resistant strains developing; some people don't complete the course of antibiotics. **(3)**

Page 20

1. **(a)** **Any two from:** to ensure that the drug is actually effective / more effective than placebo; to work out the most effective dose / method of application; to comply with legislation. **(2)**
   (b) Double blind trials involve volunteers who are randomly allocated to groups – neither they nor the doctors / scientists know if they have been given the new drug or a placebo **(1)**; this eliminates all bias from the test **(1)**.
   (c) (i) Total patients = 226; $\frac{21}{226} \times 100$ **(1)** = 9.29% **(1)**
   (ii) Yes, there are more patients who took the drug and had a cardiovascular event than those who took the placebo. However, there is not a large difference between the groups. **(1)** No, the cardiovascular events could include other conditions apart from heart attacks. **(1)**
   (iii) Rash **(1)**; the difference in numbers of patients who got a rash between the alketronol and placebo groups is quite large **(1)**.

Page 21

1. **(a)** **Mineral deficiency:** lack of nitrates **(1)** **Leaf appearance:** yellow leaves and stunted growth **(1)** (Also accept **Mineral deficiency:** lack of magnesium / potassium / phosphate **(1)**; **Leaf appearance:** chlorosis / discolouration of the leaves **(1)**)
   (b) There is a high concentration of *Chalara* cases in the East of England ✓ **(1)**
   (c) (i) **Any two from:** burning trees destroys fungus / *Chalara*; prevents further spores being produced; reduces spread of spores. **(2)**
   (ii) **Any one from:** not all trees removed; trees may produce spores before being detected / destroyed; more spores could be introduced by wind from mainland Europe. **(1)**

COORDINATION AND CONTROL

Page 22

1. homeostasis **(1)**; receptors **(1)**; effectors **(1)**
2. **(a)** Negative feedback **(1)**
   (b) (i) It reduces production of ACTH. **(1)**
   (ii) **Any one from:** ineffective nutrient distribution; inability to reduce inflammation; inefficient water control. **(1)**
   (iii) Patient D **(1)**
   (iv) 5 × 7 = 35 μg per litre **(2 marks for correct answer; if answer is incorrect, 1 mark for showing working)**

Page 23

1. **(a)** Nucleus **(1)**; **(b)** Cell body / cytoplasm **(1)**
2. **(a)** Brain **(1)**
   (b) A means of detecting external stimuli, i.e. a **receptor (1)**; transferral of electrical impulses to the CNS, i.e. a **sensory neurone (1)**; a coordinator / control system, i.e. a **brain (1)**.
3. **(a)** Synapse **(1)**
   (b) **Any three from:** transmitter substance released at end of first neurone in response to impulse; travels across synapse by diffusion; transmitter binds with receptor molecules on next neurone; nervous impulse released in second neurone **(3)**.

Page 24

1. **(a)** Cerebral cortex / cerebrum **(1)**
   (b) The brain contains junctions between all three types of neurone ✓ **(1)**
   The brain is part of the central nervous system ✓ **(1)**.
2. **(a)** **Any two from:** muscle contraction; generates heat; through respiration. **(2)**
   (b) **Any two from:** evaporation of sweat from skin; requires heat from body; radiation; endothermic change. **(2)**
   (c) 37°C **(1)**

(d) Blood vessels / arterioles narrow **(1)**; blood shunted below adipose tissue / fat layer **(1)**; fat insulation reduces heat loss from blood. **(1)**

Page 25

1. **(a)** A3 **(1)**; B1 **(1)**; C2 **(1)**; D4 **(1)**
   (b) Light rays fall on the **cornea** where they are refracted / bent **(1)**; the **lens** then refracts / bends light further **(1)**.
2. Caused by an eyeball that is too long / weak suspensory ligaments that cannot pull the lens into a thin shape **(1)**; corrected using a concave lens **(1)**.
3. Bobcats are likely to be able to form more detailed images in bright light / have better colour vision **(1)**; because cone density is greater **(1)**; cannot conclude that they have better night vision as data about rods is not available **(1)**.

Page 26

1. **Gland:** pancreas **(1)**   **Hormone:** insulin / glucagon **(1)**
2. **(a)** **Any two from:** after meal, a rise in glucose levels will be detected by device; which will cause hormone implant to release insulin; insulin released to bring blood glucose level down. **(2)**
   (b) People with type 2 diabetes can often control their sugar level by adjusting their diet **(1)**; body's cells often no longer respond to insulin **(1)**.
3.

Gland	Hormones produced
Pituitary gland	**TSH, ADH, LH** and **FSH** (accept any two)
Pancreas	Insulin and glucagon
Thyroid gland	Thyroxine
Adrenal gland	Adrenaline
Ovary	**Oestrogen** and **progesterone**
Testes	Testosterone

(1 mark for each correct line)

Page 27

1. **(a)** 1600 ml **(1)**
   (b) Amounts are equal **(1)**; important that water intake should balance water output to avoid dehydration **(1)**.
   (c) Intake of water greater **(1)**; output from sweating greater **(1)**; water gained from respiration greater **(1)**, as muscles contracting more / respiring more **(1)**.
2. **(a)** B **(1)**
   (b) C **(1)**
   (c) A **(1)**
   (d) Low water levels in blood detected by receptors / in blood vessels / in brain **(1)**; more ADH released by pituitary gland **(1)**; acts on collecting duct / kidney **(1)**; which is stimulated to absorb more water back into bloodstream **(1)**.

Page 28

1. Days 5–14: uterus wall is being repaired **(1)**; egg released at approximately 14 days from ovary **(1)**; days 14–28: uterus lining maintained **(1)**.
2.

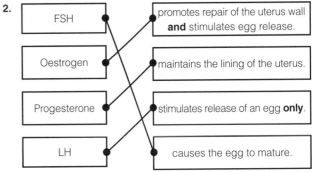

(1 mark for each correct line up to 3 marks)

3. (a) Negative feedback **(1)**
(b) FSH **(1)**
(c) Progesterone **(1)**
(d) Continues to be produced **(1)** in large quantities / at high levels **(1)**.

Page 29

1. (a) Leroy and Jane **(1)**
(b) Three: Tim and Margaret, Rohit and Saleema, and Leroy and Jane. **(1)**
(c) Although irregular ovulation has a lower success rate **(1)**; it affects over twice as many couples (16×75 produces a larger total than 7×95). **(1)**
(d) Both methods mean that Jane does not make any genetic contribution **(1)**; egg donation has a high rate of success but can be expensive **(1)**; surrogacy might be cheaper but there is a risk that the surrogate mother might develop an attachment to the baby / want to keep it **(1)**; egg donation requires invasive technique **(1)**.

2. Any two from: the contraceptive pill contains hormones that inhibit FSH production; e.g. oestrogen / progesterone; eggs therefore fail to mature; progesterone causes production of sticky cervical mucus that hinders movement of sperm **(2)**.

Page 30

1. The shoot grows upwards and root grows downwards when the bean germinates **(1)**; after it is turned, the shoot shows negative geotropism / gravitropism and grows upwards **(1)**; the root shows positive geotropism / gravitropism and grows in same direction as force of gravity **(1)**.

2. Plant hormones ✓ **(1)**

3. This is a model answer, which would score the full 6 marks:
Miriam would take 50 seeds, all of the same mass and planted at the same time. These would be grown in the same compost in a large tray with an equal spacing of 5 cm between each seed. The seeds would be placed in an enclosed chamber with a single lamp source shining from one direction. A similar tray could be placed in a chamber where the light was entering uniformly from all directions. This would be the control. Over the next five days, the compost in both trays would be supplied with a known dose of water to ensure that it was kept moist. At the end of a five-day period, the seeds that have now grown shoots would be removed. A count would be made of the number of shoots that were leaning significantly away from the vertical towards the source of light. It would be expected that Miriam would find that most, if not all, of the shoots were pointing towards the light in the first tray, whereas the shoots in the second tray would be growing vertically. This procedure could be repeated numerous times to increase the reliability of the observations. **The answer provides all possible detail and alternatives to answer the question. In summary, you need to cover:** fair testing / controlled experiment; how the number of responding seedlings would be measured; the correct pattern in the results.

INHERITANCE, VARIATION AND EVOLUTION

Page 31

1. gametes **(1)**; haploid **(1)**; meiosis **(1)**
2. Meiosis shuffles genes, which makes each gamete unique ✓ **(1)**; Gametes fuse randomly ✓ **(1)**
3. (a) Any three from: sexual reproduction can be an advantage to a species if the environment changes; asexual reproduction is more advantageous when the environment is not changing; some organisms use both types of reproduction, therefore both have their advantages; sexual reproduction might yield disadvantageous adaptations in an individual when the environment changes. **(3)**
(b) Sexual: male and female parents required; slower than asexual; requires meiosis; more resources (e.g. time, energy) required. **Asexual:** only one parent required; faster than sexual; requires mitosis only; less resources required. **(1)**
(c) Cytoplasm and organelles duplicated **(1)**; as a 'bud' **(1)**

Page 32

1. The genome of an organism is the entire genetic material present in its adult body cells ✓ **(1)**; The HGP involved collaboration between US and UK geneticists ✓ **(1)**; The project allowed genetic abnormalities to be tracked between generations ✓ **(1)**.
2. (a) Organisms with very similar features / chimpanzee and human share equal DNA coding for protein A. **(1)**
(b) Yeast **(1)**
3. (a) Any two from: warn women about the risk of cancer ahead of time; enable early and regular screening; enable early treatment; suggest treatment that is targeted. **(2)**
(b) Other factors may contribute to onset of cancer **(1)**; risk is in terms of a probability (which is not 100%) **(1)**.

Page 33

1. (a) T pairs with A; C pairs with G **(both correct for 1 mark)**
(b) 3 **(1)**
2. (a) Any two from: UV light; radioactive substances; X-rays; certain chemicals / mutagens. **(2)**
(b) Base / codon / triplet sequence changed **(1)**; leads to change in amino acid sequence **(1)**; protein no longer has correct shape to perform its job **(1)**.
3. Stage 1: DNA unzips and exposes the bases on each strand / a molecule of messenger RNA (mRNA) is constructed from one of these template strands. **(1)**
Stage 2: The mRNA carries a complementary version of the gene / travels out of the nucleus to the cytoplasm. **(1)**
Stage 3: In the ribosome, the mRNA is 'read' / tRNA molecules carry individual amino acids to add to a growing protein (polypeptide). **(1)**
Stage 4: The new polypeptide folds into a unique shape / is released into the cytoplasm. **(1)**

Page 34

1. (a) 39 **(1)**
(b) Black is the dominant gene / allele; white is recessive **(1)** **(no marks given for references to 'black chromosome' or 'white chromosome')**; the allele for black fur is passed on / inherited from the father **(1)**.
(c) Correct genotype or gametes for both parents (Bb and bb) **(1)**; genotype of offspring correct (Bb and bb) **(1)**; correct phenotype of offspring **(1)**.

	b	b
B	Bb Black	Bb Black
b	bb White	bb White

Or

B   b   b   b

Bb   Bb   bb   bb

Black   Black   White   White

2. (a)

Brown eyes   ×   Blue eyes

Parents   BB   ×   bb

Gametes   B   B   b   b

Offspring   Bb   Bb   Bb   Bb

Phenotype | Brown | Brown | Brown | Brown

(1 mark will be awarded for the phenotype row and 1 mark for offspring row.)

(b)

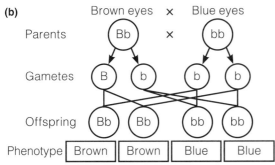

Parents   Brown eyes × Blue eyes

(1 mark will be awarded for the phenotype row and 1 mark for the offspring row.)

Page 35

1. **(a)** 205–215 million years ago **(1)**
    (b) (i) Cretaceous **(1)**
        (ii) They have discovered fossils. **(1)**
    (c) Lizard **(1)**
    (d) Archosaur **(1)**

Page 36

1. **(a)**

Before Industrial Revolution		After Industrial Revolution	
Pale	Dark	Pale	Dark
1260	107	89	1130

(1 mark for mean numbers before Industrial Revolution; 1 mark for mean numbers after Industrial Revolution)

(b)

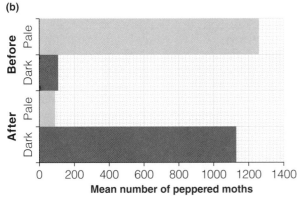

(2 marks for correct plotting of bars; subtract 1 mark for every incorrect plot.)

(c) The pale-coloured moths could camouflage themselves easily against the silver birch tree bark. **(1)**

(d) Dark-coloured peppered moths were more camouflaged than pale moths after the Industrial Revolution due to the effects of air pollution **(1)**; dark moths had an increased chance of survival and consequently an increased chance of reproducing and passing on genes **(1)**.

2. Lucy was one of the earliest known hominids to have an upright stance. **(1)**

Page 37

1. evolved; slow; adapted; genes **(4 words correct = 2 marks, 2 or 3 words correct = 1 mark, 1 or 0 words correct = 0 marks)**
2. Mendel's work showed that characteristics could be passed on from parents to offspring; studies of genetic material have revealed the unit of inheritance as the gene / DNA **(1)**.
3. **(a)** Mitosis **(1)**
    (b) It enables them to produce many plants with the same desired characteristics from just one parent plant **(1)**; it enables them to produce many plants quickly. **(1)**
    (c) If plants are susceptible to a disease or change, all the plants with those genes will be affected **(1)**; reduction in genetic variation reduces potential for further selective breeding **(1)**.

4. **Any one from:** embryos can develop into healthy human beings and the rights of the embryo / potential life have to be addressed; at some stage the embryo is able to suffer pain and at this point it would be unethical to experiment on it. **(1)**

Page 38

1. **(a) Any three from:** Allow chosen males and females to mate / breed / reproduce together; select offspring from several matings that have high quality wool; allow these sheep to mate together; repeat the process over many generations **(stages must be in sequence). (3)**
    (b) Any one from: high quality meat / lamb; thick coat; hardiness / ability to withstand harsh winters; colouration / markings; disease resistance. **(1)**
2. **Any two from:** involves genes, not whole organisms; genes transferred from one organism to another; much more precise in terms of passing on characteristics; rapid production; cheaper than selective breeding; (or reverse argument). **(2)**
3. **(a)** Crops containing soya can be sprayed with herbicide so weeds are killed rather than soya. **(1)**
    (b) Rice produces carotene, which provides poor populations with vitamin A. **(1)**
4. GM plants may cross-breed with wild plants, resulting in wild plants / weeds that are herbicide-resistant. **(1)**

Page 39

1. **(a) Underline any one of the following**; carnivorous big cats; five toes on their front paws and four toes on their back paws; claws can be drawn back. **(1)**
    (b) Leopards are more closely related to tigers **(1)**; both are the Panthera genus / snow leopards are a different genus **(1)**.
2. **(a)** Possesses features that are found in reptiles and birds **(1)**; feathers place it with birds but it also has teeth / does not have a beak like reptiles – it is an intermediate form **(1)**.

ECOSYSTEMS
Page 40

1. features; characteristics **(either way round for features or characteristics)**; suited; environment; evolutionary; survival **(6 words correct = 3 marks, 4 or 5 words correct = 2 marks, 2 or 3 words correct = 1 mark, 1 or 0 words correct = 0 marks)**

2. **(a)**

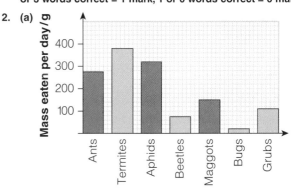

(2 marks for correctly plotting bars, 1 mark for correctly labelling x axis.)

(b) $\frac{380}{1330} \times 100 = 28.6\%$
(1 mark for correct answer, 1 mark for showing working)

(c) It occupies more than one habitat / niche **(1)**; eats a wide variety of food / prey **(1)**.

Page 41

1. **(a)** Habitat **(1)**
    (b) Ecosystem **(1)**
    (c) Any one from: pooter; sweepnet; light trap. **(1)**
    (d) 16 × 4 × 5000 = 320 000 **(1 mark for correct answer, 1 mark for showing working)**
    (e) (i) Less competition for food between beetles **(1)**; numbers increase as a result **(1)**.
        (ii) Snail numbers would decline. **(1)**

Page 42

1. (a) Biogas **(1)**
   (b) **Any two from:** burned to generate electricity; burned to produce hot water / steam / for central heating; used as fuel in houses; used for cooking. **(2)**
   (c) Remote areas don't have access to mains electricity; burning biogas can generate electricity. **(1)**
2. (a) Tube D **(1)**; because it is warm and moist **(1)**.
   (b) The soil / air / surface of the leaf **(1)**
   (c) So that air / oxygen can get in **(1)**
   (d) **Accept one from:** they could count the number of whole discs left at the end; they could record what fraction / percentage of leaf discs decayed and find an average; they could measure the percentage decrease in mass of discs by measuring mass before and after time in soil. **(1)**

Page 43

1. Water; wind; wood **(1)**
2. **Climate zones** shift, causing ecosystems and habitats to change; organisms are displaced and become extinct. **(1) Sea levels** rise, causing flooding of coastal regions; islands are inundated and disappear beneath sea level. **(1) Ice caps and glaciers** melt and retreat, resulting in loss of habitat. **(1)**
3. (a) See graph **(2)**
   (b) Millions (Also accept billions) **(1)**

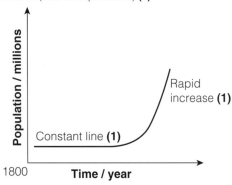

   (c) **Any two from:** insufficient birth control; better life expectancy; better health care; better hygienic practice. **(2)**

Page 44

1. **Any two from:** climate change; new predators; habitat destruction; hunting; competition; pollution. **(2)**
2. (a) Cutting down large areas of forest ✓ **(1)**
   (b) Increase in atmospheric carbon dioxide ✓ **(1)**

3. **Any two from:** provide land for agriculture; road building; mining; construction. **(2)**
4. tropical; trees; carbon dioxide; biodiversity; extinct; habitats **(6)**
5. Nutrients in the soil are absorbed by crops and are not replaced. **(1)**

Page 45

1. (a) Chemical energy ✓ **(1)**
   (b) $\frac{1000}{6000} \times 100 = 16.7\%$
   (2 marks for correct answer; if answer incorrect, allow 1 mark for $\frac{1000}{6000} \times 100$)
   (c) Cellulose in plant material requires more energy to digest **(1)**; so larger amounts need to be consumed **(1)**. Accept converse argument for humans.
   (d) **This is a model answer, which would score the full 6 marks:**
   Shorter food chains are more energy-efficient because they have fewer trophic levels. A vegetarian food chain may have only two levels: plants – humans, whereas a meat-eating diet will have three or more. We know that energy is lost at each trophic level as respiration, heat, excretion, egestion and movement. In this way, a consumer may lose up to 90% energy and only pass on 10% to the next consumer in the chain. Producing food for a vegetarian population requires decreased areas of land because at least one trophic level is removed from the food chain. A field of wheat will feed many more humans than a field of cattle. This can be seen in a pyramid of biomass, where the width of the human trophic level is greater when humans are a primary consumer compared with when they are a secondary or tertiary consumer.

Page 46

1. (a) 160 thousand tonnes (plus or minus 10 000 or in range 150–170) **(1)**
   (b) Overall decrease in numbers **(1)**; temporary rises in 1988–1993 and 2003–2006 **(1)**.
   (c) (i) 1907 tonnes **(1)**
      (ii) Numbers of haddock still declining **(1)**; therefore less fish should be caught in order for fish stocks to recover **(1)**.
   (d) **Any one from:** increasing mesh size to allow young cod to reach breeding age; increase quotas of other fish species. **(1)**

Question number		Answer	Notes	Marks
1	(a)	Lactic acid		1
	(b)	Carbon dioxide		1
2	(a)	Her muscles can release more energy.		1
	(b)	**Cause:** build-up of lactic acid (in muscles)		1
		Recovery: heavy breathing / panting		1
		over a period of time		1
	(c)	**Any three from:** More blood to the muscles. More oxygen supplied to muscles. Increased energy transfer in muscles. More lactic acid to be removed from muscles.		3
3		cell, tissue, organ, system		1
4		White blood cells		1
5	(a)	Right ventricle		1
	(b)	Blood is pumped at a higher pressure. / Blood is pumped a greater distance.		1
	(c)	They stop the backflow of blood.	Allow: they stop blood flowing in the wrong direction.	1
	(d)	$\dfrac{22\,100}{105\,650} \times 100 = 20.91812\%$ 21% to two significant figures		1 1
	(e)	**Any two from:** Low(er) fat intake Low(er) salt intake Regular exercise Healthy body weight Low stress levels		2
6	(a)	It's a physical barrier – prevents pathogens from entering. It produces antimicrobial secretions (peptides) to kill microorganisms.		1 1
	(b)	640 <table><tr><td>Time</td><td>Bacteria</td></tr><tr><td>0</td><td>10</td></tr><tr><td>20</td><td>20</td></tr><tr><td>40</td><td>40</td></tr><tr><td>60</td><td>80</td></tr><tr><td>80</td><td>160</td></tr><tr><td>100</td><td>320</td></tr><tr><td>120</td><td>640</td></tr></table>	Allow 1 mark for: number doubles six times in two hours.	1 1
	(c)	Measles is caused by a virus. Antibiotics only treat bacterial infections.		1 1
	(d)	$\dfrac{10}{5000} = 0.002 \times 1000$ $= 2\ \mu m$		1 1
	(e)	**Any two from:** Boil / sterilise all water. Isolate infected individuals. Any basic hygiene measure involving water.	Allow: wash hands / toilets away from water supply, etc.	2
	(f)	There is less chance of contracting the disease as it reduces possible contact with infected people. The disease cannot spread as people are immune.		1 1
7		Cell wall		1

8		**Any four from:** Sterilise wire / inoculating loop in flame. Transfer sample of pond water to agar. Seal lid with a cross of tape. Turn upside down (to stop condensation). Incubate at 25 °C.		4
9	(a)	Moral / religious / ethical reasons (e.g. use of embryos to obtain stem cells, it interferes with natural processes, 'plays God' or is against religious beliefs) Possibility of virus transfer		1 1
	(b)	Differentiation		1
10	(a)	**Any two from:** Guard cells fill with water by osmosis. Guard cells change shape. Guard cells become turgid.		2
	(b)	The net movement of particles from an area in which there is a high concentration to one of low concentration. **Any one from:** The (random / net) movement of particles. Particles spread out / particles mix up.	Allow molecules instead of particles.	1 1
11	(a)	**Any two from:** Long Thin Tubes / hollow / no end walls		2
	(b)	**Any two from:** Thin cell wall Large surface area Long, hair-like structure		2
12	(a)	To stop evaporation (of the water)		1
	(b)	2.5 cm³ per day $$\frac{50-40}{4}$$	Allow 1 mark for: total volume lost = 10 cm³	1 1
13	(a)	39		1
	(b)	Mitosis **Any two from:** Chromosomes are copied. Two full sets of chromosomes are made. Each set moves to the opposite end of the cell. **Any one from:** Cell divides in two. Each new cell contains a complete set.		1 2 1
14		Bacteria reproduce very quickly. They form clones / exact copies of the DNA. Bacteria DNA is easily altered / plasmids easily modified.		1 1 1
15		**Any three from:** Smoking Obesity Viruses UV exposure Excessive alcohol intake		3
16	(a)	Amylase		1
	(b)	(Plant) protein broken down by enzymes / protease into amino acids. Amino acids reassembled into new protein.	Allow 1 mark for: 'by enzymes' for reassembly if not credited for breaking down.	1 1 1 1
	(c)	Enzymes are denatured at 60 °C. So proteins / fats from food are not broken down.		1 1
17		**Any three from:** Starch – for storage Fat / oil – for storage Cellulose – to make cell walls Amino acids – to make protein	To score a mark, both the substance and reason must be noted.	3

18	Water has moved / diffused into sugar solution		1
	from a dilute to a more concentrated solution.		1
	Visking tubing is partially permeable.		1
19	Make up 'acid rain' solution (e.g. a dilute sulfuric acid or nitric acid solution, or a solution with a pH in the range 2–6).		1
	Minimum of two groups of infected roses – spray one group of roses with acid solution.		1
	Control variable, e.g. same place in garden.		1
20	Stops it from being eaten		1
21 (a)	Less growth / growth will be stunted		1
(b)	**Advantage** – good supply of nitrate		1
	Disadvantage – large number of rabbits needed to obtain enough manure to treat field		1
22 (a)	Higher temperature leads to faster growth.		1
	More carbon dioxide leads to faster growth.		1
(b)	$6H_2O$		1
	$6O_2$		1
(c)	**Level 3:** Correct patterns for linking both temperature and distance to *rate* of photosynthesis. Explanations linked to light intensity, energy and enzymes.		5–6
	Level 2: One correct pattern / prediction outlined for both distance and temperature. One correct explanation linked to one pattern / prediction.		3–4
	Level 1: One correct pattern / prediction outlined for either distance or temperature. One correct explanation linked to the pattern / prediction.		1–2
	No relevant content		0
	Indicative content **Patterns / predictions** • Fewer bubbles / less photosynthesis with increasing distance • More bubbles at 35 °C • Fewer / no bubbles at 55 °C • Rate of photosynthesis decreases with increasing distance • Rate of photosynthesis increases with temperature up to around 45 °C • Photosynthesis stops at higher temperature **Explanations** • Increase in distance reduces the amount of light • Less light, less photosynthesis • Higher temperature up to around 45 °C – more photosynthesis • More energy increases photosynthesis • Rate of photosynthesis decreases with decrease in light intensity • Correct mention of inverse square law • Rate of photosynthesis increases with increasing energy • Above 45 °C enzymes are denatured and so little or no photosynthesis		
23 (a)	B		1
(b)	The pathogen is disabled / dead / weakened.		1
24	**Any two from:** Viruses are found inside cells. Damaging a virus also damages cells. Viruses have a high mutation rate.		2
25 (a)	Enzymes are proteins.		1
	Monoclonal antibodies target one specific binding site on the enzyme.		1
	The activity is reduced because the binding site on the enzyme is blocked.		1
(b)	**How:** Use of a placebo with some patients.		1
	Why: Removes any bias that may be present in a blind trial, where the doctors know who has the placebo drug.		1
	This is because no one knows who has the real drug.		1

Question Number		Answer	Notes	Marks
1		A		1
2		Disease		1
3		**Any two from:** Small ears (reduce heat loss) Thick fur (reduces heat loss) Thick fat / blubber (reduces heat loss) Sharp claws (for holding onto prey) Hair on pads of feet (to grip ice)		2
4		$\dfrac{15 \times 21}{4} = 78.75$ 79 (nearest whole number)		1 1
5	(a)	**Any one advantage from:** Ability to control temperature. Ability to control food / high protein food. Easy to catch. It is sustainable. **Any one problem from:** Disease spreads easily. Attracts fish predators. People have ethical objections to this method.		1 1
	(b)	Fishing quotas Control of net sizes		1 1
6	(a)	*Strigops*		1
	(b)	Primary consumer		1
	(c)	**Any three from:** Evolution needs mutations to occur. Mutations are rare. Mutations are usually harmful. Advantageous characteristics are not always selected for. Time is needed for even small changes to occur.		3
7		Less resistant bacteria are killed first / survival of the fittest. If course not completed, resistant bacteria survive. Resistant bacteria then reproduce.		1 1 1
8		The method of formation of other types of rock destroys the remains of the organisms.	Allow specific examples: e.g. the high temperature of igneous rocks destroys the remains.	1
9		**Any two from:** There was not enough evidence at the time. The mechanism through which variation was passed on was not known. It challenged religious beliefs.		2
10		Control of movement		1
11		D		1
12		As body heats up: sweat is produced blood vessels dilate / vasodilation. As the body cools rapidly in the icy cold water: sweating stops / shivering starts blood vessels contract / vasoconstriction / hairs stand up.		2 2
13		Muscles change the shape of the iris. Pupil smaller / less light into eye. Muscles stretch lens. Light focused on retina / back of eye.		1 1 1 1
14		Stored in an atmosphere of ethene gas		1
15	(a)	Shoot grows against gravity / negative geotropism / negative gravitropism. Auxin / growth hormone on lower side of shoot. Lower cells elongate / grow more.		1 1 1
	(b)	Inhibits cell growth / reduces growth on lower side of root.		1 1

16	(a)	Any figure in the range 12.9–15.		1
		Trend – darker colour to more mass loss.		1
		Darker colour – higher temperature / faster decay.		1
	(b)	**Any two from:**		
		Grass from same place		
		Same mass of grass cuttings in each bag		
		Same material for bag		
		Same thickness of material for bag		
		Same thickness / packing of material in the bag		2
17	(a)	Female reaction time better than male / females have faster reaction time than males.		1
	(b)	$\dfrac{0.31 + 0.32 + 0.29 + 0.32}{4}$		1
		Answer is 0.31		1
	(c)	Rapid / fast		1
		Automatic / done without thinking		1
	(d)	Impulse causes release of chemical / neurotransmitter from ends of sensory neurone.		1
		Chemical / neurotransmitter diffuses across gap.		1
		Chemical / neurotransmitter binds to receptor molecules on next / relay neurone.		1
		This triggers electrical impulse in next / relay neurone.		1
18		**Any one from:**	Accept other types of scan:	
		MRI scan	e.g. TMS, EEG.	
		Electrically stimulating brain		
		Study of people with brain damage		
		Dissection of brain from dead person		1
		Any one ethical issue from:		
		Must not cause damage to patient's brain		
		Patients may not be able to give permission		1
19	(a)	No		0
		The best chance is at or just after 14 days.		1
		That's when the egg is released / level of LH (luteinising hormone) is at its highest.		1
	(b)	Maintains lining of uterus		1
		Inhibits both FSH and LH		1
	(c)	**Any two from:**		
		They inhibit FSH.		
		No eggs mature (and they cannot be fertilised).		
		Progesterone causes production of sticky mucus, which hinders movement of sperm.		2
	(d)	**Any two from:**		
		Success rates are not high		
		Can lead to multiple births		
		Multiple births have a risk for mother / babies		
		Very stressful		2
20		Bean plant from seed		1
21		**Any one benefit from:**		
		Produces many plants quickly		
		Rare plants can be preserved		
		All plants have desired characteristics		1
		Any one disadvantage from:		
		No genetic variation		
		All plants may be susceptible to disease / change		1
22		Select the cows and bulls that have the milk qualities required.		1
		Breed them.		1
		Select the offspring that have the best milk qualities.		1
		Repeat over a number of generations.		1
23		**Any two from:**		
		Other effects on human health not known		
		Concerns about effects on other crops		
		Concerns about effects on insects / wildlife		2

24	(a)	Allele		1
	(b)	Emily and Georgina		1
25	(a)	A = 27%		1
		C + G = 46% (100 – (2 × 27) = 46%)		1
		C and G = 23% (46 ÷ 2)		1
	(b)	T, T, A, G, A, T, G, T	They must all be correct for 1 mark.	1
	(c)	3 amino acids		
		3 pairs of bases code for		
		1 amino acid		1
		9 base pairs = 3 sets of		1
		3 base pairs		1
26	(a)	Both parents: Ff		1
		Four offspring: FF Ff Ff ff	Upper and lower case letters must be distinguishable.	1

	F	f
F	FF	Ff
f	Ff	ff

26	(b)	25% or 1 in 4		1
	(c)	Heterozygous		1
27	(a)	**Level 3:** Correct descriptions of all four control methods.		5–6
		Level 2: Correct description of control method 1 **and** one other control method (2, 3 or 4).	Allow 3 marks for a full description of methods 3 and 4 only.	3–4
		Level 1: One correct description of any control method.		1–2
		No relevant content		0
		Indicative content		
		Control method 1		
		Pancreas monitors glucose level		
		Pancreas produces insulin if glucose level high		
		Glucose converted to glycogen		
		Glycogen stored in liver / cells		
		Control method 2		
		Pancreas produces glucagon if glucose level low		
		Glycogen converted to glucose by glucagon		
		Control method 3		
		Type 1: blood glucose levels tested regularly		
		Insulin injections if glucose level high		
		Control method 4		
		Type 2: diet control		
		Regular exercise		
	(b)	**Any two from:**		
		They:		
		filter the blood		
		remove water from the blood		
		remove ions from the blood		
		reabsorb glucose into the blood		
		reabsorb water into the blood		
		reabsorb ions into the blood.		2
	(c)	Proteins broken down to amino acids.		1
		Excess amino acids form ammonia (in liver).		1
		(Toxic) ammonia converted to urea.		1
		Urea removed by kidneys / less protein – less urea.		1
28		Burning trees produces more carbon dioxide in the air. /		
		Less photosynthesis means more carbon dioxide in the air.		1
		Carbon dioxide is a greenhouse gas / causes global warming.		1
29		**Any two from:**		
		Stabilises ecosystems		
		Preserves food chains		
		Preserves possible future crops		
		Preserves possible future medicines		
		Preserves interdependence of species		2
30		**Any one from:**		
		Maintains the ability to produce indefinitely		
		Does not damage the Earth for future generations		
		Can carry on forever		1